M000047555

Inside the Minds of Car Dealers

How to Buy Your Next Car Without Fear

by

Ray Lopez

Five Star Publications, Inc.
Chandler, AZ

Linda F. Radke, President
Five Star Publications, Inc.
P.O. Box 6698
Chandler, AZ 85246-6698

www.InsidetheMindsofCarDealers.com

Library of Congress Cataloging-in-Publication Data

Inside the minds of car dealers : how to buy your next car without fear / by
Ray Lopez. — 1st ed.
    p. cm.
  ISBN-13: 978-1-58985-156-6
  ISBN-10: 1-58985-156-0
 1. Automobile dealers—Vocational guidance. 2. Deals. I. Ray Lopez
  HF5439.A8I57 2009
  629.222029—dc22

                                      2009013931

Printed in the United States of America

Cover Design by Kris Taft Miller

To Sean Durrie, thank you for your relentless work and support in writing this book.

Inside the Minds of Car Dealers

How to Buy Your Next Car Without Fear

If you're looking for books on how to buy a car, the market is loaded with them. They're written by salespeople who give you a few secrets on how to get a good deal. They let you think that, after you read their book, you'll know enough to counter anything a salesperson may say or do. But it's far from the truth. No salesperson will tell you everything. Why should they? After all, they make their money on conning you. They'll reveal a couple old school tactics. You believe you're armed to the teeth and you hit the dealership lot with this knowledge. In reality, you just took the bait and now it's time for them to reel you in.

You'd be surprised at how many people are involved in getting you to buy a new car. It's not just the salesperson and the sales manager. Did you know the deal actually begins with the owner and ends with the lot attendants? They, and every person in between at the dealership, are involved in psychological ploys to get you to want that new car.

It's a more complex game than you imagine. It's in the wording of their ads and in the way they display the cars on their front line. Even the placement of the dealership showroom in relation to the street— and to the service department—play a vital role in piquing your appetite to buy.

They all make their living off what you don't know. For instance, do you know the first place you should begin shopping for a new car? No, it's not the Internet, the showroom, or car magazines. It's a place you'd never think of. But salespeople know where it is. And none of them will ever tell you. Until now.

I spent almost 30 years selling cars. I retired in 2006. Now I want to educate you on every way we work you, play you, and bury you when we sell you a car. I'll take you through the entire sales process from the minute you walk on the lot to the moment you sign the contract. I'll even break down the contract for you so you'll know exactly what you're signing and initialing. I'll let you know what each person at the dealership does to help close the deal.

But before I get into how to begin your research, I feel it's vitally important to give you an insight no other book will give you. You need to understand what happens the moment you drive up to a dealership lot. Like the machinations of what we do before we even greet you. How we steer you into a car and then into a sale. We guide and you follow. Why? Because we are *always in control.*

You need to break through this control if you ever want a fair deal. And the only way to do that is to educate yourself on the psychology of the dealership, the salesperson and the sales process.

Introduction

The only thing worse than getting an audit from the IRS is shopping for a new car. No matter how badly you need or want a car, just the thought of having to step onto a dealer's lot is enough to make you sick. For decades, the stereotypical salesman has been a schlock, balding guy in a loud plaid suit. He's smoking a fat, stinking cigar and trying to talk you into buying that "hot seller" before he runs out of them. Of course, he's got ten more just like it in storage.

Things got so bad that in 1958, Senator Maroni had to create legislation that required all auto manufacturers to paste a suggested list price on every new car. The car's ID number and every option on it had to be listed plainly on a window sticker. Option prices, base price, and transportation price had to be included in the bottom line called the MSRP, or manufacturer's suggested retail price.

Today, things have changed somewhat. The Internet supplies a lot of useful information. You are now better educated when you shop for a new car. But the blue-suede-shoes salespeople are still around, working at high-pressure dealerships. The Internet doesn't prevent a schlock salesman from burying you in your purchase. Just as it's changed the way you buy a car, it's also changed the way that these types of salespeople con you.

Buying a car is laborious and intensive. You need to know what salespeople know and how they think. You need to polish your act before you ever set foot on a dealer's lot. You need to learn how salespeople counter everything you say to get you to buy right here and now. And you need to know how a dealership functions. Without having that valuable insight into the way a dealership is set up and how the layout works to make a sale, you'll always be at the mercy of the sales staff. That includes the salesperson, the closer, the sales manager, the used car manager, and the finance manager. It can also include the service and parts managers, as well as the porters.

Once you learn how each of these people affects the sale, you'll be able to negotiate with them in a calm, orderly, and businesslike manner. You won't lose your temper—that's very important. By staying level-headed, you keep thinking clearly and sensibly. You'll end up with a fair deal from start to finish.

Wouldn't it be great if, just once in your life, you could have the dream car-buying experience? It would go something like this: You walk on the lot. The salesperson gives you time to look over a few cars before he greets you. He introduces himself and asks what you'd like to see. He listens to everything you say and cordially takes you to a car that matches your desire.

He tells you only about the features that matter most to you. He knows his product inside out and has an answer for every question you ask. He politely asks about your purchase time frame. His attitude is friendly and sincere. During the test drive he's quiet so that you have a chance to take in everything about the car. Back at the dealership, you talk it over and he listens attentively. If you're not ready to buy just yet, he gives you initial figures and lets you leave with his card. If you're ready, he gives you the very best price right up front. He explains how the sales manager arrived at this price and why it's the best they can do. He's honest and friendly. You trust him. You buy the car and feel great about it. After you sign the contract, both of you shake hands. You've just made a new friend.

We know that just doesn't happen. And it sucks because if it did, you wouldn't dread going to a dealership. You wouldn't come onto the lot with a chip on your shoulder, or be so afraid that the first time he asks a question, you run back to your car and burn rubber getting away.

CHAPTER 1

The Uneducated Buyer

I've sold cars for over 30 years. Although many of them have been the high pressure, turn-over dealerships, I've been fortunate to work at reputable and honest dealerships since 1998. Rydell Automotive in the San Fernando Valley is a rarity. They're a best price dealership. Every car is clearly marked with the lowest discount price so you know immediately what a car will cost you. There's no up-selling or hidden cost. And there's no haggling. It's all been eliminated by their best price policy. The Auto Gallery in Woodland Hills, Ca. is another dealership of integrity, selling high-line vehicles such as Ferrari, Maserati, Porsche, and Audi. Places like these may be rare, but they do exist.

At these dealerships, I was thoroughly trained to treat everyone as though they were my immediate family. Lying, exaggerating, and cheating were grounds for dismissal. But for many years before I came to them, I was your worst nightmare. I didn't wear loud plaid suits or smoke fat cigars. But I would sell my own mom and dad if the price was right! I could con you into a car without you even knowing it. I made it seem like you outfoxed me and you bought it just to spite me.

It didn't matter that you weren't ready to buy or couldn't afford the car. I set out the bait and you bit. And I bragged to the other salesmen about my commission off your deal. For two decades I lied, double-talked, exaggerated, and pressured you into anything I wanted to sell. I should've been in politics—I probably would've been president by now!

What I really fed on was when you'd bring somebody with you to negotiate so you wouldn't get ripped off. Or when you'd tell me you knew all about sales strategy and you couldn't be talked into anything. Or better yet, when you'd say you did a lot of research online and read some books on how to buy a car. By telling me this up front, you just gave away your entire game plan. You left yourself wide open for me to attack you from every angle. I made my best commissions off people like you.

One thing I realized right away is that most people buying cars share one thing in common: contradiction. You hate shopping for a car more than anything else, yet you'll eagerly drive onto my lot. You despise the shady, schlock, high-pressure salesman, but you'll stay for hours on end at my desk and let me coerce you into a car and payments you won't be happy with. You want to be treated fairly, yet you don't want an honest salesperson because you wouldn't trust him. And if you do get up and start to walk out, the second I call you, you'll turn back and stay for more abuse. Why? *Because you want to be lied to.* There's no other reason. From the moment you turn back, I know I have full control over you. You think you've caught me and now I'm going to come clean and give you a real deal. Yeah, right!

A schlock salesman is not only a wonderful psychiatrist; he's also a great actor. I act contrite and maybe apologize. You bite and eventually leave in a car that I just made a fortune on! Even today, with all the available information on the Internet, you still get harangued and pressured into a car with payments you really don't want.

So how do you stop this madness? How can you buy a car as simply as you'd buy a new pair of shoes? EDUCATE YOURSELF! Knowledge is power. But it takes a lot of learning. I'm going to do my best to teach you everything I learned over 30 years of selling cars. That's a lot of information.

Buying a car is not easy. Neither is gaining decades of knowledge in just a few pages. That's why this book is thicker than most others on how to buy a new car. But once you've read it through, you'll have much more knowledge than anyone else shopping for a car. You'll be amazed at how a dealership functions. So many things are put into motion, from when you first step on our lot, until you leave with your new car. It's not just me pouncing on you. It's the entire dealership!

CHAPTER 2

Getting a Fair Deal

Since 1971, I've worked in every department of a dealership: service, body shop, parts, and sales. I know how a dealership functions. I'm retired now. I don't have to sell anymore. Before 1998, I did things that make me sick when I think about them now. But a situation occurred at a high-pressured dealership that turned things around for me.

It was actually more like an epiphany. I was working at a high-line import store. These cars ranged from relatively pricey to ridiculously expensive. By the time I'd been there three weeks, I had already sold seven cars—an impressive start for any luxury car salesman.

My brother came in to buy a used Mustang GT convertible I had taken in trade. He had been looking for one and I knew this one was in good shape. I wrote him up as a house deal plus $500—more than enough to cover paying everyone involved in the sale and still make something on the deal. The sales manager came out and congratulated him on getting such a great deal. He mentioned that I had made a lot of money for the company since I started and was the number one salesperson for the month.

Once my brother drove off, the sales manager called me into his office and ripped into me. He was screaming so loudly that everyone on the sales floor heard him. I'll never forget how he ended his tirade. He said, "We're here to make money on everybody! You steal every last dollar you can get. And if you can't f___ your own family and brag about it afterwards, you don't belong here!"

That was a cold slap of reality across my face. I went to the glass display case where our sales licenses were, smashed it with my shoe, took my license, and told him to f___ himself!

A day later, I was at Rydell Automotive using their best price policy. I went on to sell Audis at the Auto Gallery until I retired.

Integrity is what made the difference at those two dealerships. Things are changing in the philosophy of car-selling. Some dealers now want their salespeople to be consultants—to listen to you and help you—not loud, high-pressure, plaid-suit-wearing, fat-cigar-smoking liars. But what if there aren't any dealerships like these near you? How can you keep from getting buried?

To start off, you need to know some dos and don'ts. Then I'll give you a lesson on how and where to begin your research, followed by an insider's view of the sales process. Finally, I'll walk you through a detailed step-by-step sale with a blue-suede-shoes salesman.

DOS AND DON'TS

- DON'T ever give away your ace in the hole by mentioning this book.
- DON'T ever mention your research on the Internet or say that "you're onto us."
- DON'T ever shop for a new car when your emotions are high.
- DON'T ever lie or make excuses. Salesmen know them all and will use them against you.
- DON'T ever shop one dealer against the other. You'll always end up losing.
- DON'T ever try to insult a salesperson. We're immune to it and will use it against you.
- DON'T ever think you can outfox or out-negotiate. We do this for a living.
- DON'T ever say you know exactly what they paid for the car you want. The salesman will find a way to prove you wrong and humiliate you.

- DON'T expect to get a dealer's very best price until you're ready to buy.
- DON'T give any salesman the time of day if they're not listening to you. Walk out and don't look back.
- DON'T ever turn back if you're walking out.
- DON'T listen to anything they're saying to get you to stay.
- DON'T let anyone stop you from leaving. Just keep walking to your car and drive away! Turn back and the salesman will grind you up like hamburger.
- DO all your research before you visit the dealership.
- DO feel knowledgeable and be alert.
- DO be pleasant.
- DO be honest with the salesmen, even if we're not with you.
- DO accept the fact that the dealership is a business and is entitled to make money like any other business.
- DO accept the fact that your trade-in is not worth what you think it is.
- DO ask me to work on just one element at a time, not all of them at once—for instance, the price of the new car, your trade-in value, monthly payment, and down-payment.
- DO expect me to know my products inside-out.
- DO expect me to listen to your wants and needs.
- DO expect me to be professional at all times.
- DO tell me, in a professional manner, if I ever make you uncomfortable.

   And most importantly . . .

- DO your negotiating intelligently and sincerely. You'll get a fair deal and so will the dealership.

I say "a fair deal" because a dealership is a business. There's rent, payroll, taxes, utilities, insurance, storage, and inventory to pay every month just like any other business. They're entitled to make some profit. But not to rip you off. A fair deal is one that gives you a decent price on your new car and allows the dealership to make something on it too. Everybody wins.

CHAPTER 3

The Science of Selling

When people ask me what's the best book to read on buying a car, I tell them to read one on selling cars, not buying. You'll learn so much more from those books on what we do to get you hooked on a car, and how we close a deal.

A lot of blue-suede-shoes salespeople are never satisfied with just selling cars. They also want a position of prominence to massage their egos. Some become sales managers. Others may become used car dealers. And still others want to be the published author of the ultimate book on selling. They want to brag that their book has sold more copies than any other "how to" book and that it's inspired so many other salespeople to become successful. In them, they boast of how they buried someone in a car. That's also known as "a full boat deal." What they didn't count on was how greatly it helped the buyers who read the book, who then went to the dealership and got a fair deal without all the lies and heavy pressure.

But all those "how to sell" books leave out some very important subjects: the sales secrets that made those salesmen a fortune. They worked for years to figure them out. So why would they want a "green pea" (new) salesman to have that advantage and compete with them for the almighty dollar? That's why this book is different: I'm retired. I no longer fight for "ups" on the lot. I don't need to hustle you out of every last cent you have. I'm no longer in the dog-eat-dog world of car sales. And I'm free to divulge everything to you.

There's a science to selling. It involves sizing you up from the moment you drive in. As a blue-suede-shoes guy, I'd instantly break you down into one of five types of buyers. Then I'd decide which one of the four types of personalities you have. I'll describe these types in detail later on so that you don't go into "information overload."

Once I've established this, I know exactly which head games to play and how to lead you into sweetening my paycheck. I ask qualifying questions, making sure that every question is "open-ended." You can't answer with just a simple yes or no. You have to elaborate, giving me more information than you intended. For instance, I don't ask you, "So you like this car?" Instead I ask, "What do you like about this car?" Open-ended questions are designed to get you to open up and start selling yourself on the car. For every feature you ask about, I'll show you the benefit of it. This starts to get your temperature warmed up.

Then I let you sit behind the wheel. I show you a few options and let you try them. Your emotions are stirring. I let you start it up. You're becoming anxious. We go on a test drive—but I drive it off the lot. I drive it first. This ploy is as old as dirt. I've used all the excuses: "It's due to insurance liability." "It's the law." "I have to warm it up." Whatever! But the truth is that every dealership uses this trick for one reason only: to whet your desire to drive the car and build your temperature into a fever. Everything else you're told is B.S. Keep this to yourself!

On the test drive I don't say anything. I let you experience the sensation of owning. I let you imagine the car is yours. If you have any questions, I answer quickly then continue my silence. The radio stays off unless you ask to turn it on. I turn it on for a moment then shut it off. A radio can distract your daydream of ownership. And I certainly don't want you to hear a commercial for one of my competitors!

Something else you need to know: on the test drive, I'll tell you where to turn. What you don't realize is that they're all right turns. Right turns are very easy to negotiate. Every customer, including you, feels some anxiety in driving a car that's not yours—especially if it's a new car worth $30,000 or more. That's why you're told to make only right turns. Left turns can increase that anxiety and your focus will no longer be on wanting to own the car. It'll be on how to survive a left turn and get back to the dealer pronto!

We're getting close to the dealership. You love the car and you've made only right turns. Now I start a trial close. I ask you something about the car as it relates to your hot buttons. Again, it's an open-ended question. "How do you feel about the navigation system?" If there's time, I'll ask one more before you drive back onto the lot.

Back on the lot, I make sure we do a walk-through of the service department. I want to show you how we'll take care of you after the sale. I introduce you to our service manager. He smiles, shakes your hand, and asks you what car you just drove. After you tell him, he says that it's a very good car. Hardly any problems and it's a popular seller. It doesn't matter which car you drove, he'll say that about every model we sell. It's all part of the clincher to help make the sale. Since the service manager is not a salesperson, you feel he can be trusted. So you find it easy to believe him.

As we're walking back to the office, I'll hit on a couple more hot buttons. I make it sound as if it's just an afterthought. After all, I don't want you to get wise to what I'm doing. I casually mention—mention, not ask—that the car has the equipment you're looking for. You agree. And it's in the color you want. Again, you agree. I state, "So, if the numbers are right, you'll drive it home." You agree. BINGO!

What just happened is I used psychology to get you to sell yourself the car. I played on all five senses: sight, smell, touch, sound, and taste. I showed you the car you wanted. I let you take in the new car smell. I let you feel the car from the driver's seat. I started the engine so you could hear it running. Then I whetted your appetite for it with the test drive. And notice that when we got back to the lot, I never once used the words buy, purchase, own, or *take* home. I said *drive* home. Those other words would immediately break your spell because they'll snap you back to reality—you're on a car lot and I'm a schlock salesman.

CHAPTER 4

Reality Check!

You don't know how to buy a car. Neither does your brother, sister, cousin, husband, wife, neighbor, or anyone else you might bring along to help you get the best deal. None of you know how to buy a new car the right way! The more you think you know about negotiating, the more I use that against you. Even if you do know some of my tricks, you're still at a great disadvantage.

Why? Because I'll always be better prepared than you. I do this day in, day out. Six days a week. Ten hours a day. I'm constantly polishing my act.

Here's a simple question to get this discussion started: Do you know where to start looking for a car? The Internet? The dealership? Car magazines? None of these are the right places to go.

What about your trade-in? What's its true cash value? I can guarantee you it's nowhere near what you think it is. Should you trade your car in, or should you sell it yourself?

Do you go to a national chain or a family-owned dealership? When is the best time of the month, week, and day to shop? Finance through the dealership or through your own bank? Pay cash? What about extended warranties? And how do rebates and incentives really work for you? What model and size is truly right for you and your needs? What options are necessary? What options are frivolous? What about the color? Did you consider all the important factors when you decided on the exterior and interior?

Most importantly, do you even know what you're doing? I doubt it! A harsh thing to write, even harsher to read. But it's true. So here's some insight into what we've known for years, to enlighten you.

TIME AND DAY

The best day to buy is a weekday. Traffic is generally slower than on a weekend. You'll have more time to browse and I can give you more personal time. Weekends can be like a zoo. The lot is filled with customers. My strategy is to do a quick "size up" on you. And if you don't seem like a real buyer right away, it's onto someone else. Weekends have another drawback—spiffs. We get bonuses (spiffs) every weekend for selling three, four, or five cars, along with our commission. The bonuses are always paid by Tuesday so I don't have to wait for my next paycheck. I love instant cash! So I'm going to be a lot more aggressive with you Friday through Sunday.

Weekends are also the time we advertise our weekly loss leaders. Those are the cars in the newspapers that are priced incredibly low. And they're always "1 At This Price!" That's to motivate you to visit our lot. Once you see how ugly and plain that car is, you'll want to see something better equipped. CHA-CHING! You've just up-sold yourself. And my commission increases.

Mornings are not the best time to buy. Most times, a morning arrival is an eager customer who can't wait to buy. They show up between opening and 10:00am. If you're that eager, you're a lay-down. And you'll pay sticker or very close to it, along with a whole lot of extras you didn't expect, such as an extended warranty, custom wheels and tires, and a wheel warranty. Or, on the flip side, you may not get the car of your dreams because of the limited number of salespeople on the clock. Instead, you get the one who hates being there so early in the morning. His attitude sucks. You've interrupted his morning coffee, which makes things worse. Good luck trying to get any answers out of him. And you can forget about a test drive. You leave feeling embarrassed and frustrated, and your entire day is downhill from there.

Evenings are not optimal either. If you come in within an hour before closing, I'll size you up right away. If you seem like a real buyer, I'll speed through the sales process as fast as I can, cutting corners and pressuring you more than I normally would. I may even give you an ultimatum if it gets very close to closing and you still haven't decided. I want to get home at a decent time. I can make you feel guilty for keeping me there. You buy the car to relieve your guilt.

If you drop by between 6:00 pm and 7:00 pm, that's feeding time for the sharks. We know a lot of working people can only stop in around that time. You could be home, resting. Or having dinner. Or watching TV after a long day at work. But you're here looking at a car. And that means you have an inclination to buy. It's up to me to make sure you do. The feeding frenzy begins! Maybe you had a hectic day at work, but you promised yourself you'd start car shopping. That's when I play the nice guy role. I'll tell you that you've had enough B.S. for today, so "let's just get right down to the bottom line and cut out all the fat." That makes you feel that you can trust me, which is what I want. I bait the hook and you bite!

Or maybe you're coming onto our lot in an emotional state. You've been beaten up and lied to at other dealers all day. You're frustrated. I acknowledge this and sympathize with you. Guess what? I'll end up selling you a car right at closing. You'll think I'm your new friend. I grin to show I understand it's late and that you want to get home. At this point you don't care too much about the numbers—until the next day. But by then it's too late. You own it!

But if you show up in the afternoon, you're none of those types. You're on middle ground with your emotions. Your attachment to buying a new car is neutral. You'll be mentally and emotionally fit to negotiate a fair deal. You'll get extra attention from me since that is the slowest time of day for business. I'm ready for a sale and will make a conscientious effort to actually work for you, rather than myself.

If you call ahead and set up an appointment, I'll be sure to free up my time so that I can give you undivided attention. Which brings up a sore point with us. Appointments are very important to us, even though you may not think so. Sure, we may all be a bunch of shysters, but we're still businessmen. It's how we earn a living. If you make an appointment, please keep it! If you can't make it, or if you change your mind, have the courtesy to call and let me know. Turn the situation around. How would you feel if I left you waiting at your office for hours and I never showed up? I didn't even call. Be kind enough to call.

Something else to consider about not showing up is that I'll always be in control. So if you do break our appointment and show up at a different time or on a different day, I'll remember you. I won't show you any animosity. I'll shake your hand and welcome you to our dealership and just let my pen handle the revenge.

FAMILY OWNED VS. NATIONAL CHAINS

Regarding the type of dealership you should shop, that's discussed in fine detail in the next chapter. But when it comes down to choosing between a family-owned business and a dealer owned by a national chain, go to the family-owned business. You're more likely to get personal attention with fewer high-pressured sales tactics, and your salesperson will most likely have been there for a long time. We tend to grow roots where we're the happiest.

National chains carry a huge overhead with all the dealerships they own. The board of directors and its investors put a lot pressure on them to make money at any cost. This means selling a lot of cars each month. But in order to do that, they have to have steep discounts. They must beat their competition. This, in turn, means the salespeople earn just a "mini" on each car they move out. A mini is a set amount the dealer will pay for each sale, regardless of how little profit was made off the car. It's a basic guarantee. Usually it's between $100 and $200. But salespeople earning only minis at the chain stores have to sell at least 20 cars a month to make a decent living. They're unhappy, frustrated, and angry. They'll quit the moment they find another job. Or be fired for low production. They have no stability. So, besides getting hustled at one of these types of dealerships, you'll also find out how quickly you're neglected or forgotten once your salesperson is gone. Try the family-owned dealership first.

INTERIOR AND EXTERIOR COLORS

When buying a new car, always think of resale: its anticipated worth when you trade it in a few years from now. Color combinations have a lot to do with the resale value of your car. Buying a popular color may be beneficial only if it's a neutral color, not a flashy one. For instance, silver is still one of the most popular colors for cars. A lot of people want a silver car. It's a neutral color. It's not flashy like gold metallic, green medallion, or ostrich. Even if those colors are hot today, they'll be the "what was I thinking?" colors of tomorrow. Silver is a safe bet that your car will bring you the most value when you trade it in.

Neutral colors are black, white, blue, silver, gray, and beige. Green's popularity depends on the region. Red and yellow depend on the type of car. If you do buy silver, go with a black, charcoal, or gray interior. Stay away from tan or beige interiors. They clash with silver rather than complement it. A good-looking color combination brings a better trade-in value. Something that appeals to a very limited number of people will actually cost you because the dealer is taking in something that will be hard to resell.

Try to go with a two-tone interior if it's available. It tends to break up the blandness that a single-color interior may have. It doesn't have to have contrasting colors such as red and black. It can be two shades of gray or two shades of beige. Two tones give your car personality. Just be sure that both colors coordinate with the exterior, and be sure you know what colors are in demand in your region. Check out all the late model cars you see on the highway. What are the most common neutral colors? If you want a higher trade-in value you should choose only between those colors, even though your mind may be set on gold metallic with red interior.

Here's a quick rundown of colors to help you get started. Green is still popular in the central states but it's dead in the West. At one time, dark green metallic was all the rage nationwide. Now you can't give that color away in most regions. Red and yellow are great colors on sport coupes and sport sedans, but not on other cars. The family hauler needs to be neutral. There are a few exceptions. Some mid-size and full-size family sedans look good in red, as long as it's a deep metallic and not Ferrari red. And if you must go with yellow, avoid taxi yellow like the plague! It'll kill your resale value at trade-in.

This brings up another very important point—red cars and law enforcement. It's been said for ages that a red car will get you more tickets than any other color. B.S.! Don't believe it. I've been told by the CHP and LAPD that there are so many red cars on the road that they don't stand out any more than a black, white, or blue car does. It's a myth that has no truth to it. So if you want a red car, buy it! Just avoid bright yellow. Now there's a color that does attract unwanted attention. Yellow is the first color the eye discerns. The brighter it is, the easier it is to spot immediately. As an LAPD captain told me, "We notice yellow cars right off the bat. Then it's those boy-racer tuners." Assuming then that you are not in the market for a tricked-out used Honda Civic or Integra RS, my advice on your new car is to avoid yellow and buy one of the neutral colors.

If you own a family hauler, the interior cannot be so light that scuff marks are easily left in it. The same goes for a luxury car. Who wants to pay a lot for their car, only to have it look like a work truck inside with all the stains and scuffs marks?

A light interior does work well under certain circumstances. If your car is classified as a personal coupe or the latest rage, a "coupe-sedan," then a black car with beige interior is a very good combination—and a better seller in the West and South than black over black, since that combination generates excessive heat in the summer.

The same goes for all dark exterior colors. If your car is classified a personal vehicle, you can go light on the interior without a penalty. The general rule of thumb is the interior color should always be of the same hue or lighter than the exterior. It should never be darker. The exception to this is white and beige cars. But be wise. White with beige or silver interior is a good combination. But beige over a black interior is way too much contrast for most people.

FACTORY OPTIONS—NECESSARY OR FRIVOLOUS?

Options require a lot of attention. Some are frivolous. Others are necessary. Some are bundled into a package so you must buy the entire package to get the one option you wanted. Then there are those necessary-for-trade-in-value options that will cost you huge deductions if you don't have them. Navigation is one of those options. It was nothing more than a "look at me" high-tech toy just a few years ago. Now, everybody wants it. Even if you don't use it, you need to include it in your purchase because a few years from now, when practically every car has it and your car doesn't, you'll take a heavy penalty hit when you trade in your car.

Some high-tech gadgets are purely frivolous and should be avoided. Self-parallel parking, 360-degree cameras, lane wandering avoidance, and adaptive cruise control cost way too much today and won't be worth much at trade-in. They can actually make your car depreciate more than those cars without them.

Self-parallel-parking is a waste. It takes far too much time to operate and the parameters for it to work right are very restrictive. The 360-degree camera works when you back up or parallel park. It's like having a camera mounted on the roof. But it can give you vertigo because the images are very surreal and confusing. It can cause you to misjudge your movements, rather than refine them. You'll need hefty insurance coverage with this option.

Lane wandering avoidance will either sound an alarm or cause the steering wheel to shudder if you should straddle lanes. It sounds like a great safety feature, but how practical is this? If you do all or mostly city driving and spend a lot of time in rush hour traffic, you'll never use it. And do you really need your steering wheel vibrating or a jarring alarm to warn you to stay in your lane? How about just keeping your eyes open and paying attention? That can save you several hundred in the initial cost of the car.

Adaptive cruise control is a very beneficial option—if you live in Montana. It keeps you a safe distance from the car ahead of you. If that car should brake, adaptive cruise control activates your car's brakes. If that car changes lanes, the radar attaches itself to the next car ahead. It's an extremely expensive "look what I got" option that most of us will never use because highway traffic makes it impractical. Go with this option, and you've just wasted $2,500.

Unless you can actually use these options often enough to justify their extremely high costs, they are not worth it. A word of advice: Avoid them and learn how to parallel park on your own and pay attention while you're driving. Use the standard cruise control, if you can ever find a road open enough. You can save yourself a lot of money.

Some things, like heated and air conditioned seats and heated steering wheel, are godsends. You'll use them a lot during winter and summer and they'll pay for themselves—and be greatly appreciated by the next owner.

A sunroof can be a frivolity to some and a necessity to others. When it comes to trade-in value, it will give you something back. But you won't get dinged if you don't have it. The initial cost may make you think twice about it. That's a toss-up; in the end, you must decide.

Rear-parking assist? That depends on what you're buying. Large SUVs and large cars, as well as cars with limited rear visibility, should have this. A simple thing like judging distance when you're backing up in one of these vehicles can be nerve-wracking. You don't really know how far away objects are when you're behind the steering wheel, practically 20 feet away from the back bumper. This option can help.

Electronic stability programs, traction control, and anti-lock brakes are must-haves. If your car doesn't include them in its standard equipment, buy them. Not only will you feel a lot safer with them, your trade-in value will take a good hit for not having them. The same goes for head curtain air bags. These options will be strong selling points for you when you trade in your car.

Memory seats? That depends on the car. If you buy a full-size car, a power seat is recommended. Multiple drivers can adjust it to suit themselves, and it will give you more on trade-in than a car without it. But a memory seat? Think it over cautiously. It's not a necessity on a family sedan or smaller vehicle, unless two drivers use the same car quite often. Then it's a blessing to you and well worth the cost.

THE RIGHT VEHICLE AT THE RIGHT TIME

Some of you have pipe dreams about what you want to buy. Sure, it would be awesome to drive a BMW M5—but do you need all that power? No. Do you need the monumental gas bills? No. Do you need the M5 just so you can keep up with your friends? Yeah, that's about it. But that's not practical.

That's the key to getting the right car for your needs: being practical. Most people buy more car than they need. You see a commercial on TV or an ad in a magazine. You see a car pass you by on the freeway. Or your neighbor just bought a new car that caught your attention. And now you have to have one. That's impulse buying, and we prey on buyers like you. We go into a pack-animal mentality as soon as you hit the lot and say, "I've gotta have a new 370 Z."

A 370 Z is a two-seat sport coupe. Imagine, for instance, you're an architect. You take two or three clients to lunch most days. You take blueprints home, or to a construction site. The 370 Z is not the right car for you. You need a sedan or a mid-size SUV. You're buying the wrong car at the wrong time. You're not being practical. And you're buying while you're hot for the car. Cool down and think it over wisely.

The same holds true if you "have to have," say, an Audi A8L. You're the only one who will be in the car going to and from work and to the store. But you may have a passenger or two on the weekends. The A8L is a very large car. You don't need a car that big if you're the only one who will be in it most of the time. Sure it has panache and status. But an A6 is also very luxurious, is a better fit for you, and costs up to $25,000 less!

Many times, what you want and what you need are not the same. Don't overbuy. And don't buy when your emotions are riding high. You may get stuck in a car you'll soon discover isn't at all what you thought it would be, or it's too big and impractical and you're buried in it.

CHAPTER 5

Rebates and Incentives

Manufacturers are now using terms such as Customer Cash, Customer Assistance, or Factory Cash rather than the word "rebate." They'll use anything to disguise the fact that certain models aren't selling well, or not at all. The higher the rebate, the slower it's selling. And that 6-letter "R" word has the connotation of desperation. No matter what they call it, you know it's a rebate. And you know why it's offered.

On the other hand, we salespeople know why it's offered too. We use it as a selling tool to get you hooked on buying a car that you may not have been able to buy without it. We up-sell you into a car you don't need—one we need to sell and get off the lot. Here's how it works: You come in looking at a mid-size sedan. It has a $1,500 rebate. The mid-size has a V6, power windows and door locks, and a CD player with an auxiliary port. We have a few on the lot. But we have a lot more of our full-size sedans that cost more and offer us a larger commission. The large sedans have a V8, dual power seats with leather and memory, and a six-disc in-dash CD player with auxiliary port. V8s are eating us up. Nobody wants them because of their gas mileage and the high cost of 91-octane gasoline. They may even have a bonus attached to them. If I sell one, I get an extra $200 cash, plus my commission. If I sell two, I get an extra $500 cash plus commission.

How do I get you to bite? Easy! The full-size sedan has a $4,000 rebate on it. That's a lot more than the mid-size. That's my bait to use on you. After the test drive on the mid-size, I take you into the show-room, deliberately walking you past the full-size with the generous rebate marked all over it. It's eye-appealing. You take a look and sit inside. BINGO!

I nonchalantly show you the features the mid-size doesn't have. I let you take it all in without saying a word. You're starting to sell yourself on it. You forget about the V8's gas mileage and that it needs premium gasoline. You're waiting for me to tell you that I may be able to get you this car close to the price of the mid-size. But I don't. I let you sweat for a while. It makes it easier for me to reel you in.

We go to my desk. I pull out a write-up sheet and start to figure out a deal on the mid-size. I stop, look up at you, and say I don't know what I can do on the full-size car, but if you give me a few extra min-utes, I can find out. You're drooling inside at this point. You want the full-size sedan with all its features. The key to this scenario is I let you sell yourself. Then I use the $4,000 rebate as the carrot. I never once tell you I may be able to get it at the price of the mid-size. I just keep mentioning the rebate. And I use it successfully to up-sell you into a car you don't need—a car that costs you more in ownership and will take a much bigger depreciation hit because of its V8 and size. But I don't give a damn. All I want is my bonus cash.

I constantly used rebates to up-sell to my advantage. But that's not what they're designed for. Their primary purpose is to move slow-selling vehicles. They're supposed to be used to entice you to buy the car that fits your needs by lowering the overall purchase price, or to be used with your down-payment, thus making your payments more affordable.

A word of caution: In California, all rebates have to be included in the selling price so they can be taxed. Once taxed, they're deducted from the selling price or put into your down-payment. Please check with your state laws to see if this applies.

Something else that is very important: REBATES CAN SERI-OUSLY AFFECT THE TRADE-IN VALUE OF YOUR NEW CAR! The way that works is quite simple. For every $1,000 of rebate on your new car, it will take an additional $500 hit when you trade it in, on top of its usual depreciation. For example, you want a new SUV that has a

$5,000 rebate on it. When you trade it in a few years from now, you'll take the usual depreciation hit PLUS an extra $2,500 hit!

A final word on rebates: If you must use the rebate as a means to buy the car, YOU CAN'T AFFORD IT! Downsize and buy something within your price range. Or wait until you have enough down to make the payments workable.

Now we come to incentives. This term applies to interest rate rebates. Any time you see a manufacturer offering less than standard interest rates, it's an incentive. Very often, the car you want will have an incentive and a rebate, but you can only use one of them. You have to choose which way you want to go. The best way to make your decision is to have your salesperson show you your monthly payments using the rebate and using the incentive. Be sure you use the same amount down in both examples. You want to compare apples to apples. Have him show you the total cost of the car over the length of the loan. Then add in the extra depreciation hit the rebate will cost you.

You'll find it harder to qualify for incentivized rates than for standard rates. They're only offered by the manufacturer's captive financial company, such as GMAC is with General Motors. A lender is more lenient when it comes to loaning you money at 7.9% than at 0.0% or 1.9% because the lender makes money at the standard rate of 7.9% but doesn't at the incentive rate.

CHAPTER 6

Extended Warranties and Other Dealer Options

A factory extended warranty can be beneficial if you plan to keep your car longer than the original warranty. Repair costs can be staggering if they involve the engine, transmission, final drive, air conditioner, anti-lock brakes, fuel injection, or anything electrical. Look over every available plan before you decide on one. You can choose from different ranges of mileage, length of time, and deductibles. Have your salesperson show you numbers on all of them. I'm sure he won't mind because he gets a bonus for selling them.

Be sure that the warranty comes directly from the manufacturer. Any after-market warranty can be a major headache when you're trying to get your car fixed. You may have to call in with an estimate on everything that needs to be done, and then wait for it to be approved. You may have to pay for the repairs yourself and send in the claim to get reimbursed. With a factory extended warranty, you drive in to the nearest dealer, leave your car, and it gets repaired. There's a lot less frustration involved.

Once you have the numbers on the available plans, consider the cost of a zero-deductible plan versus those with deductibles. How much do you save with the $100 deductible? With a $200 deductible? Is the savings enough to make it worth taking a deductible? That's up to you and your budget.

Wheel warranties are also available through most dealerships. It's the same as buying insurance on the wheels on your car. If your wheel gets scraped, dented, or destroyed, the warranty will replace it with only a deductible cost to you. Once again, determine if your wheels are expensive to replace. Then factor in the total cost of the warranty—how much you'll pay at the end of the term. If the total amount is between 60% and 100% of the cost of one wheel replacement, forget it. Let your own car insurance take care of it. If it's between 25% and 50%, give it some thought, but think it over carefully. If the total cost is less than 25% of the cost of one wheel, buy it.

Lo-jack is probably the best anti-theft device available. So many law enforcement agencies have Lo-jack signal-tracking monitors in their cars and helicopters that you stand a very good chance of having your car recovered within 24 hours if it's stolen. Prices vary, depending on the dealer and the type of system you want. Definitely look into this if your car happens to be one of the top twenty vehicles stolen, or if it attracts attention. Honda Civics and Accords, Toyota Camrys and Corollas, and almost any car with custom 22″ wheels are prime targets. You'll enjoy the peace of mind and your insurance company may give you a small break on your premiums.

Anything other than these items is an accessory you don't need. The main design of these add-ons is to fatten up the wallets of the finance managers who sell them to you. They make bonuses for every aftermarket option they sell. Paint sealant, body moldings, stain-free interior protection—they're all useless to you, so don't buy them! Why? Because every new car comes with a clear-coat paint sealer from the factory. It protects the paint and does a much better job than the aftermarket brands. It seals in the pores and guards against the sun's UV rays. Every new car comes with Scotchguard-treated interiors. Your carpets and seats are already well protected right from the factory. Don't buy anything else. Besides being a waste of your money, it could cause a buildup of sticky residue from the two different products not matching.

To anything else the finance manager may throw at you, tell him NO! You don't want it and you want to move on to the contract.

CHAPTER 7

The Three Types
of Dealerships

Dealerships fall into one of three categories: straight sell, best price/ no haggle, and turn-over house (T-O). I'll explain how each of these dealerships work.

Straight-sell means the salesperson will take you all the way through, from greeting you to closing the sale. It could be a pleasant experience or it may be heavy, unrelenting pressure. It's a 50/50 chance that a straight-sell dealer will treat you right and view you as a long time commitment. It's also a 50/50 chance they just want to move another vehicle and get on to the next customer.

The best price/no haggle dealer is the best type to work with. You'll find every new car clearly marked with their best discount price. The negotiation is eliminated, removing the worst part of buying a car. You know immediately what the selling price is. This type of dealership is more apt to treat you with dignity and respect. They break the stereotypical car salesman mold. Everything is fully explained throughout the process, step by step. They will give you no double talk. They want you as a long-time customer.

Be careful not to fall for a dealer's "Red Tag Sale" where all cars are clearly marked only for a weekend or another specified time. They aren't a real best price dealer and are either a straight-sell or turn-over house.

The third type of dealership is the worst, the turn-over house. This is where you get passed, or "turned over," from salesman to salesman endlessly until a closer comes in and strong-arms you into buying a car right then and there. They do anything to keep you there until you sign the contract. It works like this: I greet you, then badger and hound you with a number of questions. Don't bother answering. I'm fishing for your weak spots. My goal is to sit you in a car, get you to test drive it, then get you into my office for the write-up. If I can't get you inside, I turn you over to one of my teammates who will start the process all over again. There is no limit to how many times you'll get turned over on the lot.

Now, when we finally get you to sit down in the office, the closer or team leader comes in. This is where it gets ugly. The closer mentally and emotionally beats you into submission. He's a real pro at it. This is what he does for a living. He closes the deal.

He'll stoop to the lowest level to make this happen. One of the most successful ways to do it is the guilt trip. The closer will say something like, "You don't want any figures? You've just taken my salesperson off the floor for a couple hours and you don't want any figures?" The closer makes you feel so humiliated for wasting everyone's time that you'll feel obligated to get figures—and that gives him an open door to put you into a car you really don't want.

When we return from a test drive and I bring you inside, my closer will tell me to take the car to detail and get it ready. You object. You're not ready to buy. My closer doesn't care. In fact, he's not listening! He'll distract you away from that by going over the information on the write-up sheet. When the car is finally brought up front, you tell him again you're not ready to buy. He goes ballistic. "My porter just spent two hours detailing the car! I spent two hours doing everything I can to get you the right deal. And now you don't want to buy?"

Of course, the Holy Grail of all guilt trips is when he asks you, "If I can get you this car for $_____, you'll buy it?" It sounds like he's really working for you. But what he's actually doing is going into the sales manager's office and smiling from ear to ear. Why? He's got you hooked. Now he returns and reels you in. He says, "I got really close." He puts the write-up sheet in front of you with the manager's signature approving his deal. That puts pressure on you to commit to it. It should make you get up and walk out. It's not the figure you agreed to. But you don't. Why not? Because you want to counter-offer. BINGO!

It's now back and forth. You want another $500 off. He comes back with $50 off. And so it goes for another hour or two until you're worn down and sign the agreement. A closer is very aggressive. What if you still don't bite? He goes ballistic, quietly. He puts on an act of sincerity, "Look, I got as much off as I can. You told me we would do it at $_____. You'd drive it home. We're very close." Notice again, he said "drive it home." Not "buy." He sighs. "Okay, what if we split the difference?" The closer and I are staring at you. Twice as much guilt. That always gets a yes. You just bought a car and we just made a hefty commission off you!

Guilt and turn-over work practically every time. It's a rare exception when somebody walks out on this technique. If they do, it's because that person works in sales too. She might sell medical supplies. He may sell vacuum cleaners. But they know all about closing a deal. They'll walk out. Most people won't because they don't use these mind games every day like we salespeople do. So avoid the turn-over dealers at all cost. Or you'll end up over your head and in a car you don't like and will be paying for over the next six years!

CHAPTER 8

Where to Start

All right. Now that you've gone through Car Buying 101, you're ready to start your shopping. Where do you go first?

Auto shows are great places to begin, but be careful. Many auto shows are produced by local dealers' associations. That means there will be salespeople there from all of the dealerships in your area. They will stick to you until they get your contact info and hand you a card and brochure—or until you convince them you're not in the market.

Privately owned auto shows have a distinct advantage. Manufacturers hire and train consultants specifically for this purpose. They are not salespeople from local dealerships. They don't have any cards to hand out. They can't make any money off you. So they're not selling. There's no pressure and you can wander around at your own pace.

Whether they're put on by dealers' associations or by private parties, auto shows are great opportunities to shop every model you're interested in, all in one place. You can compare features, dimensions, prices, and your emotional attachment to each car or truck in one place. You don't have to drive all over town, wasting gas and spend countless hours going back and forth from dealer to dealer.

But what if the auto show has come and gone? What if it'll be a long time before it returns? What if no auto show is in town and you need a car soon? Before you sign onto the Internet, RESEARCH THE CLASSIFIEDS IN YOUR LOCAL PAPER. That's right, go to the classifieds, even if you went to an auto show already. Start with the Sunday edition. Why Sunday? Because that's the day that has the most ads. If your town has two papers, buy them both. More than two? Just buy the two with the most circulation.

Now that you have the classifieds, do you know where to start your research? No—not the "cars for sale" ads! Look at the help wanted ads under Auto Sales. See who's hiring and what language is in the ad itself. This will clue you in to the type of dealership it is. Now get a highlighter. You'll need to mark certain key phrases and words in the ads. Look for the following:

- The ad is in ALL CAPITAL LETTERS
- Make $_____ per month! (or $_____ per year)
- Team Leader
- Closer
- Top Performers
- Pros Only
- Highly Motivated
- Strong Sales Skills
- Proven Track Record
- Old School Way of Selling
- Rare Opportunity
- The #1 Volume Dealer

Highlight each of these key phrases or words. Ideally, you'll do this every Sunday for the next six to eight weeks, and save the classifieds. This is how you will arm yourself. You need to keep track of which dealerships will treat you like cattle and which will treat you with respect. Any dealers that use those catch phrases in their ads are heavy-pressure straight-sell or turn-over houses.

Here's why: All of them are codes we salespeople know. Those ads speak to us in a way that tells us right away about their sales tactics. You need to know how to decipher them to protect yourself. In the ads, the terms Rare Opportunity and #1 Volume Dealer mean the same thing: "We push a lot of cars out the door. Don't even consider applying here unless you can show me you can you can keep up with my best salespeople." All the other terms are sales lingo that translates into, "If you can take every last nickel from your customer on the selling price, then bury them in their payment and not think twice about it, you're the guy we want!"

Sales is a cutthroat business. Keeping up with the best requires the new guy to push and shove and claw his way to a sale. And that affects you. That means you'll be screwed in many ways—more ways than usual—just so the new guy can brag about burying you. That will make him look great in the eyes of the sales manager. Yes, that's a very cold-hearted, disgusting attitude. But it exists in too many dealerships nationwide.

Some of you are saying, "Not me. I'm too smart to be taken. No one can make me buy something I don't want, or force me to take terms I don't want." And to you I say, YOU ARE A PERFECT PIGEON TO MAKE MONEY ON!

I'm not trying to offend you. I'm trying to help you. Keep in mind, you buy a new car once every four to six years. I sell four to six new cars every week! I've perfected my pitch, responses, and double talk. I can do it my sleep. Unless you sell cars for a living, you will always be at the disadvantage at the dealership.

Keep the Sunday ads for another essential reason: employee turn-around. Make a note of which dealerships constantly advertise for salespeople. If they advertise once a month or more, that's another red flag. It means there's a revolving door there. Somebody is weak and has to go. Maybe he's the lowest man in sales at the end of the month. Or maybe it's the lowest three men in sales at the end of the month. Whatever the situation, there's a heavy turn-around in the sales force.

If you buy a car from the guy who's gone next month and you have a problem, nobody will lift a finger for you. Why not? Because they didn't sell you the car. You mean nothing to them. You're on your own. Avoid these dealerships!

Now that we know which dealerships to avoid, start paying attention to the dealerships' "cars for sale" ads in the Sunday papers. Are they full page ads? Are they in color? Do they take up more than one page every weekend? This is another red flag. Those ads cost a lot. It doesn't matter if you live in a large city or a small town, full-page and color ads are expensive. The manufacturer may subsidize a portion of them. But the dealer is responsible for paying the majority of them. And he certainly doesn't want to pay for them out of his own pocket. So he spreads the heavy costs of those ads across all the new cars in his inventory. Make no mistake about it, YOU pay for his extensive advertising when you buy a new car from him.

If the dealer uses caricatures or the phrase, "1 At This Price" in his adverting, you can bet he's got a lot of heavy-pressure, blue-suede-shoes salesmen. I know. I worked at a couple of those places. We'll turn you so many times you'll be dizzy for the next 100 years! And we'll be high-fiving each other over the huge commission we made off you.

Finally, does the dealer guarantee to get you out of your present car NO MATTER HOW MUCH YOU OWE? Run away from them. They are the biggest shysters of all!

CHAPTER 9

The Internet,
Part One

What a convenience the Internet is in buying a car. You can research as many models as you want, for as long as you want, and never leave your room! You can visit independent sites like Edmunds and Kelly Blue Book, manufacturers' sites such as Cadillac or Audi USA, and magazine sites like *Car & Driver* or *Motor Trend*. You've got enough choices to keep you busy for a while.

While touring these sites, be sure to keep this bit of information impressed in your memory: Manufacturers' websites are a commercial for them. They want to pique your desire for their brand so you become emotionally attached to their cars. Emotional attachment leads to a "must see it" attitude. They will trumpet every feature and option in a way that will make you want to test drive now! Never let your emotions get the worst of you.

But there's also a benefit to those sites. They offer you a lot of in-depth information. You can configure a car just the way you want it and get an MSRP. You can also get the current rebate and incentive information from the manufacturers' sites. You can check local dealer-ship inventories for a car just like the one you want. You don't have to drive all day trying to find it.

Independent websites give you a lot of beneficial information on practically every make and model available in the US. You can get

MSRPs like the manufacturers' sites. And you can get them for many different models without having to surf the manufacturers' websites individually. A bonus many independents offer you is the invoice as well as the MSRP of the car you're shopping. But beware—invoices vary by website and they are not always accurate! Certain things are not included in the dealer's invoice on these sites, like advertising port and preparation fees. Yes, the manufacturer charges every dealer a percentage of the actual cost of the vehicle for advertising. It usually runs $\frac{1}{2}$% to 2% of the car's cost. That helps to cover national and regional ads. The vehicle's invoice price also includes port and prep fees if it's a true import from Europe or Japan. It costs money to store them at the ports and get them ready to truck to the dealers. And the manufacturers pass these costs on to their franchised owners.

Invoice prices also change as often as rebates do. Use the independent site invoice as a guide to get you close. But don't take them as the final word.

Car comparison tests on auto magazine websites offer another view on the cars you're considering. They tell you how fast the cars accelerate and brake, how well they hold on curves, and how their features compare. But always remember that their views are strictly opinions, based on personal taste. Plus, a lot of their information really doesn't apply to everyday driving. Which car can go zero to 60 the fastest doesn't matter. Same with the top speed of a car. Both can get you a very hefty ticket if you try them. Deliberate over-steer? Controlled under-steer? Who drives to work on a race track anyway? Even though this information is exciting, it's not relevant to how you will most likely drive your car.

CHAPTER 10

The Internet,
Part Two

No matter which way you research cars on the Internet, always make your first stop www.JDPower.com. Find "Car Ratings." Then click on "Ratings Tools." Then click "Quality Ratings," "Dependability Ratings," and "Sales Satisfaction Ratings." These three categories are very important. They will give you the best insight into the way the cars compare in initial quality, three years after purchase, your experience with the dealer while buying, and afterwards in the service department.

QUALITY RATINGS

Emotional attachment is something we all look for in a customer. It makes closing the deal so much easier. It affects you and your car-buying decision. You fall in love with a car. You feel an emotional attachment to it and want it. Whether it's your first or your tenth new car, you think it's the greatest thing on four wheels. Three months later, the new car smell is gone and so is the excitement that made you buy it. Now how do you feel about it? Do you still enjoy it or wish you had never made such a purchase?

Reading the "Quality Ratings" at JDPower.com will show you other owners' reactions to their car right after the time of purchase.

The emotional ties are still strong at this point. But some cars destroy that bond right away. They quickly get squeaks and rattles the service department can't find. They get electrical glitches. They're only a few weeks old and they've already been in the service department three times for the same problem. Or they're difficult to drive because they're loaded with technological overkill. You can't easily adjust the seats, the radio, or the air conditioning without going through a maze of actions that leave you with a splitting headache. All that will be reflected in this rating.

DEPENDABILITY RATINGS

How do owners feel about their cars after they've driven them a while? This is when most, if not all, of the new car emotional attachment is over. Common sense takes over euphoria. You find things that you wish you had known before buying it. The Dependability Ratings can help you avoid buyer's remorse.

What have other owners experienced? Interior parts fall off. There's excessive wind noise at highway speeds, or there's an electrical problem the service department can't fix. Perhaps it's something as simple as always turning on the turn signal every time they activate the windshield wipers. They've lived with the car for a while. Is their passion still there, or have the gremlins surfaced and given them thoughts of regret?

SALES SATISFACTION RATINGS

This rating can be an eye opener. This response from new car buyers clues you in to their experience at the dealership. Certain models have the highest reputation for quality but suffer terribly in their Sales Satisfaction survey. Their salespeople are pushy and downright obnoxious. And they know they can get away with it. Because you will take whatever rudeness and abuse they dish out just to buy that "must have" car.

Cars that sell themselves on their high quality reputations usually mean arrogant, shyster salespeople—like I used to be will be there, ready to pounce on you on the lot, on the test drive, and in their offices. Yes, I've heard over and over again, "But the car is so trouble-free. I knew the dealer was gonna push me into options I didn't need or payments higher than I liked. I just wanted to get out of there as fast as I could so I could enjoy my new car." Yeah. And you enjoyed getting hassled, harassed, and then ripped off!

The only way those dealers will change the way they do business and start treating you with common courtesy is for you to stop buying their product. Plain and simple. Once their sales drop enough, they'll stop talking down to you and treat you with respect. No one should subject themselves to being treated so rudely.

CHAPTER 11

The Internet, Part Three

Here's where you'll find out how well new cars are built: Log on to www.nhtsa.gov. Look under "Quick Clicks" on the left side of the page. Click on "Recalls, Defects, and Complaints Databases." Every recall, by the NHSTA or the manufacturer, is listed on this site. You'll also get information on complaints and defects the NHSTA is currently investigating.

This site is MUST reading to help you evaluate all the models you're shopping, but it could be a shock to you. Some models with a reputation of impeccable quality can actually have an astronomical number of recalls. Others that have had a black eye in quality have improved greatly in recent years and have few, if any, recalls. Japanese cars are good examples of this mismatch. They have enjoyed a stellar reputation, untarnished for decades. But look at how many recalls Toyota, Nissan, and Honda have had recently.

Compare your findings on this site to their J. D. Power Sales Satisfaction survey. Does the dealer have a lot of dissatisfied customers? This is something to consider when buying your next new car.

Okay, you now have a lot of valuable information on the models you're interested in. You know what type of dealership sells them by reading the help wanted ads and sales advertisements in your local paper. You know how other owners feel about their cars right after purchase and after three years of ownership. You know how many recalls and complaints they've made too. So what's next?

Go back to www.JDPower.com. Take a look at the "Service Ratings," another important survey. How well will you be treated once the sale has been made? You will spend a good many hours at the service department over the lifetime of ownership. You'll be coming in for warranty repairs, recalls, scheduled maintenance, and normal wear and tear repairs. Your expectation of how well you'll be handled can be formed by reading this survey. And, like the recall and complaints research, you may be surprised at the results. It's so much better to be surprised now, rather than after you've signed the contract.

Www.Edmunds.com is your next stop. Click on "New Cars," then on the makes and models you're interested in. Before you price them out, go to "True Cost to Own." This is a guide that takes into consideration depreciation, insurance, fuel, and maintenance costs as well as other factors. They're calculated at 15,000 miles per year over a five-year ownership. Because cost to own involves variables, such as the rising or decreasing cost of gas, and the fact that cars depreciate more in some areas of the country than others, this is just a guide. Don't take it as the ultimate word in cost. But use it to help you discover which of the cars you're shopping for may give you the better deal after five years.

Once you've done that, print out the information. Then click on the models you're interested in and begin pricing them with the equipment you want. Be sure to read the invoice price too. But always remember, the invoice price shown is not always accurate. It's a guide and nothing more.

All right, you've got your numbers. Now click on "Incentives and Rebates." This will give you the up-to-date information on most makes and models. A few do not offer any incentives. They're in black print. But the rest that do have financing and/or rebate cash have links that will open up a page showing you everything the manufacturer—and the dealer—is offering you!

This brings up a very important matter: the "trunk" money, also known as "Marketing Support" or "Dealer Cash." This is something you won't find on the manufacturers' websites. It's an incentive the manufacturer pays the dealer on certain models, once the report of sale is made. Dealers have the option of keeping it or using it to sweeten their deal with you. They are under no obligation, by the manufacturer or any local, state, or federal law, to pass it on to you!

Of those dealers who do acknowledge the trunk money, very few will give you all of it. Most will keep part of it to help offset operating costs. Again, you must realize that a dealership is a business. They need to make money to keep the lights on and pay their employees, just like every other business. If a dealer gives you any part of the trunk money, which he should as a sign of good will, consider it a little extra gift you wouldn't normally get. Think of it as a nice perk for knowing about it beforehand.

All right, let's get back to the invoice. Other websites will give you this information besides Edmunds. The same applies to them—they are not precisely accurate. But they're good guides to have. Other sites may include "Dealer Holdback" in their invoices. This is something completely different from Marketing Support. Marketing Support is put on certain models that are slow-selling. It helps to relieve the national inventory of them. Dealer Holdback is what the manufacturer pays the dealer on every car it sells, regardless of rebates or incentives. This payment can be paid per quarter or annually. No matter how it's dispensed, this money belongs to the dealer! Not you.

The dealer uses this money to help offset the flooring costs on its cars in inventory. Flooring is "rent" that the bank or lending institution charges the dealer on money the dealer borrows to buy its cars from the factory. Dealers take out loans based on projected inventory turnover, or how quickly they estimate they can sell their cars. The quicker they can turn over their inventory, the quicker they can repay the loan and save on flooring costs. But if a car remains unsold for more than a month, flooring costs can really add up. It's similar to paying interest on interest, much the same way late payments and over-the-limit charges can quickly accumulate on your credit card.

Flooring can get very expensive. That's why dealers rely on Holdback: to help offset this charge. It's their money! A word of caution, if you start negotiating by demanding the Holdback, you'll piss off the salesman and the sales manager. And you'll either be shown the door, or we'll gouge you in financing. Why? Because you're demanding that we work for free. That's right. You want us to give you everything and make no money at all on the sale. Would you work for free? I didn't think so. Don't ask us to either!

CHAPTER 12

The Internet, Part Four

A h yes. Now we're at the really fun part of buying a car: your trade-in value. What's your car worth as a trade-in? Nowhere close to what you think it is. I can guarantee that in blood.

Before we get started on the dirty work, let me emphasize that the best way to work a fair deal is to let the salesman know up front that you have a trade-in. Every book and news article you've ever read tells you to keep this out of the picture until after you get your numbers on the purchase price and interest rate. It's supposed to get you more money for your car. B.S.! By waiting until the end to tell me, I know that you read that somewhere and I'll go into overdrive to get you on the interest rate or on the selling price. All I have to do is stroke your ego. I'll say something like how you're a shrewd buyer, and then watch for a smirk on your face. BINGO! The ego stroke worked and you're getting screwed!

The smartest way to negotiate a deal is to tell me what you're trading in before we take a test drive. When we get back, I'll start filling out an appraisal sheet and give it to my used car manager. By the time we're done working out a price on your new car, he'll be back with his number on your trade-in. If I'm a decent salesperson, not a blue-suede-shoes seller, I'll appreciate your frankness and will go a bit further than usual to get you a fair deal. And you'll appreciate the fact that you cut out at least 30 to 45 minutes of staying at the dealer by having your appraisal done while we negotiated. On the other hand, if I'm Shady Sam, the schlock salesman, tell me up front about your trade anyway. Then deal with me in the way that I'll show you later in this book.

Something else I can't express loudly enough: NEVER trade in your car if you're upside-down in it! If you have negative equity, you'll just compound the problem by having me, a swift talking, blood-sucking salesperson, show you "how easy it is to get you out from your current car." This is a rule you need to tattoo on your forehead in day-glo colors—IF I'M MORE THAN $1,000 UPSIDE-DOWN IN MY TRADE, I AM NOT FINANCIALLY ABLE TO BUY A NEW CAR!

If you owe $1,000 or more than your trade-in value, you can't afford a new car if you have to trade it in to make the deal. You'll be paying much more than the new car is worth. In order to get you out from under your old car, the dealer will have to raise the cost of the new car by the amount you are upside down. It's illegal for a dealer to show negative equity on a contract!

Here's an example: Your trade-in value is $10,000. You still owe $12,500 on it. The sales manager has to raise your trade-in value by $2,500 on paper. On the contract, he'll show you were given $12,500 for it. This way it'll be a wash and no negative equity will show. In actuality though, he's only giving you $10,000 so he has to raise the selling price of your new car by $2,500 to balance out the bump on your trade. Now you're paying more in state tax, license fees, and loan interest, along with the actual cost of the car. Sure, you got your new car, but it'll end up costing you about $8,000 more over the term of the loan than if you had equity in your trade-in. Yes, $8,000 more. Not the $2,500 he raised it to get you out of your trade-in.

That has a major impact on the break-even point of your car's value and the loan. If you weren't upside-down, you could have equity in the car by the 49th month of a 60 month loan. But by financing the inequity and the resulting penalties for doing that, you won't see a breakeven point until the 60th month, if your car's value holds up.

The rule of thumb is, if you're $500 or less upside-down, go ahead and get your new car. The penalties won't hurt. If you're $501 to $999 upside-down, think it through very thoroughly. It could end up biting you at the end. Are you $1,000 or more upside-down? FORGET IT! You'll be buried in your new car for the full 60 months of the loan.

Okay, back to the appraisal of your trade-in. Every one of us who owns a car thinks ours is in the best condition. We overvalue it. Proof of that point is in the way you grade your car on the trade-in websites. Their choices are usually excellent, very good, fair, and poor. It's amazing how many of you claim your car is "Excellent"! Excellent means it's in showroom condition. It's no different today than when you originally bought it. Unless you drove it straight home and professionally stored it in a hyperbaric, controlled chamber, your car is NOT excellent.

Same goes for "Very Good." Very few cars meet the criteria. But you believe yours does. Yours just happens to be that one rare beauty that stands out from the thousands of other models just like yours. Yeah, right! What about the door dings? Or pits in the windshield? What about the worn tires? Worn brakes? What about your wheel covers or alloy wheels? Do they have a wheel rash from hitting the curb? And what about the swirl marks in the paint from car washes? Or worse, you've had body and paint work done after an accident. Forget it. Yours is not "Very Good."

Use "Fair" when appraising your car online. 95% of all cars fall into this category. It's the most honest evaluation of your car. Once you get your price, subtract another $500. Now you won't be stunned or horrified when you get the dealer's appraisal.

The reason for going back $500 from suggested trade-in value is easily explained. Your car needs more reconditioning than you think. It could be mechanical, electrical, or paint and body. For instance, you may not hear a water pump grinding or a power steering pump squealing. But a trained ear can pick that up. Used car managers are also mechanics. They know what to listen for and what to feel for while driving your car around the block. They may find something you aren't aware of.

As I explained earlier, exterior and interior colors also make a difference in your car's value. The final judgment to make on color is whether your exterior and interior create a desirable combination. Consider not just whether they look good together, but whether they attract the eye right away. For instance, a pearl-red Cadillac CTS with silver leather looks good—but a pearl-red CTS with charcoal interior shouts, "Hey, check me out!" Wrong colors and color combinations can mean a $50 to $500 hit.

If your trade-in has been in an accident, a used car manager can quickly find that out with a paint meter. It's a tool he runs across the sheet metal to gauge the paint thickness. Thinner paint means body repairs have been made. A Carfax report will also expose any major body work done to your car. On this website, used car managers can research your car for accidents, liens, true mileage, and clean title.

If your car has been in a major collision, one which required over $4,000 in repairs, you should subtract 50% of the repair costs from the trade-in value. A major collision makes your trade-in much harder to re-sell. Does your car also have frame damage? Lop off another $2,500—if the dealer will even take it. Most won't take a car in trade if it has frame damage. It will never run right, and the dealer will have a lot of liability issues to contend with.

What's your mileage? That plays an important role. If it's between 75,000 and 99,999, subtract $750 more. Your trade-in will be wholesaled to an independent used car lot. 100,000 or more? It's anybody's guess as to how much to deduct. Even some wholesalers will refuse to take a car with that many miles on it. But take an additional $1,000 hit for a total of a $1,750 penalty for miles and you may get a dealer to take it.

Why are we so harsh on body damage and mileage? Would you want a car that was in a major accident? No way. Would you trust a car that had 100,000 or more miles on it for another four years? Absolutely not. What if it has 75,000 miles? Highly unlikely. These cars are known as throw-aways. We don't want them. And you certainly don't either. That's why you want to dump it on us and get something new.

Now, if it means we have a deal with you on a new car by taking your old one in trade, the used car manager may bite the bullet and buy it. But if it doesn't have a direct effect on making a deal, don't be surprised if the sales manager wants to keep it out of the deal and let you take it back home with your new car.

On the other hand, what if your car has low mileage? That doesn't matter if you trade it in. We will never give you that additional bump that websites show for low miles. But we'll certainly try to get it when we resell it. That's just the nature of the car business.

This brings up another key element in putting all your information together before you approach a dealership. It's called honesty. You certainly don't want anything to do with a deceitful, lying, conniving salesperson. The same goes for us. We don't want anything to do with you if you try to pull a fast one on us. Be honest. We have so many ways to research the history of your car. And if we find you've been less than truthful, you'll either be shown the door or we'll find a way to bury you in the deal.

The two websites most often used for getting your trade-in value are www.KBB.com, www.Edmunds.com. Price yours out on both. You'll see how each one appraises it at a different price. That's because they're in the information business, not in the car sales business. They're not at the dealership or at auction houses buying used cars every day. They can't sell you a car. They won't buy your car. They can only gauge what they think your used car should be worth. But a sales manager works with every make and model, day in and day out, whether it's on the lot or at the auction.

Prices change all the time. A sales manager knows what your car is worth TODAY. Edmunds and Kelly Blue Book's information can be months old by the time you use it. In praise of these two websites, I must congratulate them for doing an almost superhuman job. Trying to keep up with all the data that flows in and out every day, and formulating it into figures the public will understand, is truly Herculean. They are not precise, but they will give you a ballpark view of your car's worth as a trade-in. Once again, use this information as a guide and not gospel.

With all your Internet research results, you're just about ready to tackle the most difficult part of all, visiting the dealership. But before you do, go over everything you've found. Look over every bit of research you've done. Does it look as if every dealership you need to visit is on your "Avoid At All Costs" list? Then you may want to do all your preliminary shopping by the Internet since every dealer now has an Internet department. It can save you a lot of wasted time and grief.

Even so, once you visit the dealership after the Internet contact, you still need to use everything you've learned in this book to save you from getting up-sold or buried in car price or payment. If the Internet manager uses percentages, such as "All of our cars are just 3% over invoice," tactfully tell him you want to see the invoice when you meet. If he refuses, refuse to meet him. You should try your best to get 1.5% to 2.5% over dealer cost on any vehicle. That will give you a very good deal that you can be proud of.

CHAPTER 13

On the Lot, Part One

This is the part that makes most people cringe. You'd rather turn around and head home than walk onto a dealer's lot. Nightmares and hallucinations plague you before you even get out of your car. Your heart pounds. You break into a sweat. Your knees shake and your teeth chatter.

But wait! You have a lot of valuable information already at your fingertips. You've done your homework. So take a deep breath and let it out slowly. Relax. It's going to be a lot less painful this time around.

You've got a list of dealerships you want to visit. But you need to be sure that you haven't overlooked anything before you park your car and walk onto the lot. Perhaps the dealer didn't advertise for salespeople; he relied on word of mouth instead. You might have missed out on a word or phrase that could have signaled that this dealer is a high-pressure house. Maybe their ad led you to believe this is a respectable straight-sell dealer, or the Internet manager made you believe it will be an easy, no-pressure sale. How do you know for sure if it is?

To find out, simply drive by on a weekend. Don't stop. Just drive by slowly. Look for these important elements:

- Salespeople standing just outside the showroom
- Salespeople standing alone in certain points on the lot

- Salespeople wearing white long-sleeved shirts and ties
- Balloons tied to the cars
- Hoods opened on the front line cars

Any of these indicators are sure signs it's going to be rough sailing once you're on their lot. Salespeople standing outside the showroom indicate high pressure. These people are "calling" the customers who drive up to the lot. One salesperson might call, "White sedan." Another may call, "Grand Am with chrome wheels," which is what you happen to drive, a white Grand Am Sedan with chrome wheels. Once you get out of your car both of them will pounce on you for your attention—and your wallet.

The call system is the old blue-suede-shoes way of selling cars. It's a way we compete for you and we'll stop at nothing to "call" you. Ours is a true dog-eat-dog world. And you are our dog chow.

Another reason we're standing outside is not only to call, but because we are not allowed in the showroom unless we're bringing a customer in to our desk for a write-up. The sales managers at these dealerships treat us like slaves. No respect, no dignity, just degradation. And we will treat you with the same disdain. Always remember the old saying, "S___ rolls downhill."

Salespeople standing at certain well-placed positions on the lot indicate the same thing as salespeople standing just outside the show-room. Everything that applies to that type of dealership applies to this type too. We stand alone at "points." Points are geographically noted places on the lot that provide the best view of incoming customers. I'll call you before you even pull onto the lot. I want to be the first to greet you. And I'll pull every trick in the book to make sure the other salespeople don't beat me to you.

White long-sleeved shirts and ties—if anything screams old-school way of selling, this is it! White shirts say, "I'm a heavy hitting pro. I can sell ice to Eskimos in the dead of winter!" For some reason, this type of dress is an old tradition of the super-shyster salesman. This guy personifies the typical used car salesman with a big gut, a big stinking cigar in his mouth, and a plastic smile on his face. His quick double talk and pushy tactics make you cringe and you may want to hit him.

Or spit on him. Preferably with a chaw of tobacco to stain his clean white long-sleeved shirt!

Tying balloons to the cars is also a tradition going way back to when dealers acted like circus barkers. They'd do anything to get your attention and get you into their big tent, the showroom. Once you were inside, they'd let the lions loose on you. Today, more shoppers are becoming savvy about buying a new car. Yet some dealers still think it's 1955 and operate that way.

The front line cars, which are their flashiest or hottest selling models, are washed and waxed, beckoning you to stop in and take a look. Back in the '50s and '60s, sales managers would also raise the hoods on them. They believed this would catch your eye, making you want to stop and take a look under the hood. After all, no guy would pass up an opportunity to show off his car knowledge to his wife or girlfriend—or show up the salesman. That worked to some degree back then. But we're in the 21st century! If a dealer is still stuck in the old blue-suede-shoes method of selling, you want no part of him. If you see any of these dealerships, drive away as fast as your car can take you.

Is it finally time to visit the dealers, now that you've done a visual tour? Yes, but not to shop. You have two final inspections before you're ready for that. The first, you stop in. Yes, actually get out of your car and walk on the lot towards the showroom. But walk on as a guy who wants to use the bathroom, not as a buyer. If a salesperson greets you on the lot, tell him you're looking for the bathroom. He'll direct you to the showroom.

What if a salesperson in the showroom greets you? Tell him you're going to use the bathroom. Then ask if the parts department is open today. Why ask the salesperson in the showroom about the parts department and not the one outside? Because if I'm outside, I have to keep my eyes peeled for the next customer. I have to be quick on the draw to call first. So I won't give you a second thought. But if I'm inside the showroom, my job is to work the floor. That means I'll be on you as soon as you leave the bathroom. I have to try anything to get you to take a look at a new car because you're in my "territory." But if you tell me you want the parts department, I'll leave you on your own because buying parts means you're fixing your old car—keeping it. You have no desire to buy a new one. You're a "cold fish."

Remember, I'm a salesman. I'll only focus my attention on you if you seem to have any interest in a new car, no matter how slight. So this ruse frees you from my solicitous eyes. And you're in the showroom at your own leisure! Take a visual inspection while you're in there. Do you see an office area on a raised platform? It could be just one step above the sales floor or several steps above. It's always an open space, meaning the walls are only three or four feet high, with desks and computers inside, along with some sales staff. How about any offices on the second floor with tinted windows looking down on the sales floor? Either one of these two styles tells you this is a high-pressure, turn-over house.

An open office area on a platform is known as "the tower." This is where the sales managers stand and watch everything going on in the showroom and outside. They're like wolves just waiting for the right moment to pounce on their staff or on a reluctant customer. A tower usually means this place has "closers." You'll get hammered by the closer, then by the sales manager, until you agree to sign on the dotted line.

Offices with windows overlooking the showroom floor are like super-elevated towers. The managers watch from their perches and do the same thing as those in a tower. Avoid these types of dealers at all costs so you don't end up hating yourself for getting screwed—and hating the car you just spent $30,000 on. Don't forget, with the interest rate you got nailed on, that $30,000 will end up costing you closer to $50,000 by the time you've made your final payment.

What about the sales desks? Are they in an open area or are they walled off from each other? An open area represents a more relaxed atmosphere with less stress. Walled-off offices indicate the blue-suede-shoes way of selling. It's to intimidate you, once you enter and the door closes. You no longer have any bargaining power. A major RED FLAG!

A long bench is also telling you to leave and never come back to this place. Dealers who apply serious pressure on you use this technique to sell cars. The showroom floor has no separate tables. Everyone who comes in for a write-up sits at a single long bench. The idea is that by seeing others make a deal and hearing their excitement, you don't want to be the only one there not getting a car. So if I come back and tell you your credit is a bit rough and hit you with a higher payment than you expected, you'll still take it because you don't want to be humiliated in front of everyone else.

Maybe your credit is good and you have your significant other with you. But the payment is more than you wanted. You'll still take it because it's even worse being embarrassed in front of someone so close to you, let alone a bench full of strangers.

Or you might give me an ultimatum, your last desperate try at negotiating. You tell me that if I can get it for $_____ a month, you'll take it. It's still enough to allow me to make a very good commission. So I go through the act of making it look like it won't fly with the sales manager. You sit there waiting, looking at all the other deals being done around you. After letting you sweat enough with your counter-offer, I come back with our counter-offer. It's still more than you wanted to pay. But you sign it without hesitation. You want to be a new car owner too.

What is the lesson here? If you see a bench, second floor offices over the showroom, or a "tower," don't ever come back. Not even to use the bathroom!

Now, before you leave the showroom, check for the hours of operation. Usually, they're posted on or near the main entrance. If you don't find them, go back home and look them up on the Internet. This is important. The hours of operation for the sales department are also clues to the type of dealership it is. So far, you've found a couple dealers that may be straight-sell and fair, according to the help wanted ads. You check out their layout and everything still looks fine. No tower. No second floor spy windows. No bench. And when you drove by earlier, the salespeople were milling about in golf shirts, not standing at attention like sentries in white long-sleeved shirts. So far, so good.

But now you discover that they open at 8:00 am and close at 10:00 pm. RED FLAG! As I mentioned before, only two types of salespeople are typically at a dealership that early or that late (although there are exceptions). And neither of them are the type you want to deal with. The late shift salesman will be so negative that he'll waste your time and anger you. He won't go out of his way because he isn't interested in helping you buy a car. All he's interested in is watching the clock and finding a new job with shorter hours. The early bird will get to work at 7:30 am and work the service department, hoping to find somebody who'd rather buy a new car than spend money on repairs. At 8:00 am, he's on the lot, grinning and licking his chops like a lion on a rabbit. And if you wander onto the lot at any time he's there, you are fresh meat to him.

The dealers that have extended hours don't want to miss a potential customer. "Slam as many customers into new cars as you can" is their motto. And it's Mr. Shyster Salesman's motto too. And beware of the late shift guy who's over eager to help you, unlike the late shift clock watcher. He'll catch you off guard if you should happen to stop by in the evening. From 8:00 pm on, you are a prime target. Here's how it works.

You get there between 8:00 pm and 8:30 pm. You don't feel pressured to leave because they're open an hour longer than other dealers. He keeps you looking at cars until after 9:00 pm. That's when he turns on the guilt in nonchalant ways. Like watching the sales staff locking up cars. He glances at his watch and mumbles something like, "There's still twenty minutes left—what are they doing?" Then he smiles at you and tells you to take your time. He'll stay for as long as it takes because he likes you. Yeah, right. The watch glance is a clever way to make you feel obligated to hurry up and buy. He's already convinced you that he's your friend so you'll probably reply with something like, "You've got a family waiting for you. So let's do this: If you can get me this car for $_____, we have a deal." CHA-CHING!

You just gave him a blank check. Another tactic to elicit guilt is to have the sales manager page the sales staff, reminding them that he needs to see them before they leave. Or he'll page the porters to start locking up. This gives you a sense of urgency. You begin to worry and Shady Sam, the blue-suede shoes man, turns on the good-guy smooth talk. Once again, he'll tell you he'll stay for as long as it takes. He calms you down and even offers you some coffee. And he can be almost assured of a sale because of the psychological warfare he's playing against you.

Avoid the frustration, fear, and aggravation of car shopping by embedding all these tips on researching the dealers in your head. Reread them as many times as you need until these subjects are second nature to you:

- Auto show
- Auto Sales and Help Wanted Ads
- JD Power
- Edmunds
- Kelly Blue Book
- Drive by the dealers
- Use their bathrooms, parts department
- Showroom set up
- Hours of Operation

You're almost ready to start your adventure in car buying. But you have just one more observation to make before you're ready to hit the lots and start negotiating: How many dealerships are owned by each dealer in the area? For instance, "Jones' Auto" may own a Chrysler, Toyota, Mazda, and Volkswagen dealership in the same area. This is another RED FLAG! Why? Because Jones' Auto has a very high overhead and advertising bill each month.

None of these car franchises are related. They have no employee crossover. In other words, each car line must be in its own separate building with its own mechanics, sales force, business office, service and parts department, and porters. No one can work in two or more. A single owner who has three or four unrelated car lines on the same street has an awful lot of overhead to pay. And guess how he makes all the extra money to keep the lights on? Yep, on you!

Here's a list of the "family brands" that can be under one roof—and as a result can save money for you and the dealer:

1. Buick, GMC, Chevrolet, and Cadillac
2. Ford and Lincoln-Mercury
3. Chrysler, Jeep, and Dodge
4. Porsche and Audi

None of the other makes can do this. They have to have their own stand-alone lots. Ford also owns Volvo and Mazda, yet they must have separate showrooms and sales forces for each of those brands. Even Toyota and Scion must be separate dealerships.

Be sure to make a note of how many non-related or stand-alone brands a dealer owns. This increases his overhead tremendously. Avoid all of them if you want to get a fair deal. This also applies to any publicly owned national auto dealer chains. You see their advertising everywhere, including on the trunks of their cars and license plate frames. The parent company name is always somewhere on the car. These companies not only have a huge overhead, they're also publicly traded and are beholden to their board of directors and investors to show a profit. Some of them own more than 200 dealerships nationwide of all brands. They need to cut corners every way they can to boost profits off each car they sell. They have a tremendous obligation hanging over their heads.

One of the ways to make more money off their cars is to screw us as well as you! They'll "pack" each car in inventory with a certain dollar amount. For instance, a new car may have a $300 pack. This means that the first $300 of profit is not eligible for my commission. It goes entirely to them. Then they'll make another 75% off the balance of profit and give me the remainder. This pack cuts into my commission. They pick up even more profit when they finance you. But I don't get any part of that. So at most, I'll make "minis," set figures that can range from $100 to $250 per sale.

Taxes eat into my commission. So does medical insurance. Then I have to consider all the cost-of-living factors. I need to sell at least 15–20 cars every month to make ends meet—and to appease my bosses so I don't get fired. I'm under the gun every day, every month. These types of dealerships breed bitter employees. Do you really think I'm on your side or care at all about what you want to spend? I work for a publicly owned national chain. I'm going to shove you into a car at a price that will give me more than the minimum. And then maybe I will qualify for a month-end bonus—if I sell enough cars.

Consider this: When the economy goes south, big ticket items like cars are the hardest hit. If a national chain's stock price takes a nose dive, stock holders get very nervous. They call for the CEO's head if he can't improve things ASAP. If the CEO is on thin ice, he puts unbearable pressure on those lower down in the food chain. We, the sales force, are the very lowest. Guess who gets the worst of it? And how will

I treat you the moment you step on the lot? I can guarantee you I won't bow and be at your beck and call!

As I mentioned before, independently owned single dealerships are always the best way to go when you buy a car. This includes the independently owned "family brand" dealerships too.

CHAPTER 14

On the Lot,
Part Two

Whew! I've given you a lot of information so far. And you thought you already knew how to buy a car the right way. I don't mean to rub salt in your wound. I just need to emphasize the importance of my advice. Okay, let's do another quick run through on your check list. So far you've:

1. Gone to the auto show, if possible.
2. Read the Sunday classified ads under "Auto Sales" preferably for six weeks.
3. Checked the dealers' weekend ads for size, phrasing, and color vs. black and white.
4. Researched on the Internet for cars you're interested in.
5. Researched on the Internet for the trade-in value of your car.
6. Driven by the dealerships on a weekend afternoon.
7. Inspected the showrooms under the ruse of using the bathroom.
8. Checked the hours of operation.
9. Checked for the number of non-related dealerships owned by the same company.

Now you're ready to hit the pavement as a buyer. The first thing I want to make you aware of is how most dealerships are set up. New cars are displayed on one side of the lot, used cars on the other. And in between them, on a raised area, is the showroom. It's on a very subtle rise from the rest of the lot so as not to attract attention to it. But it sits higher for a reason.

Some dealerships want a small sales force that mainly "works the floor." We're required to stand guard in the showroom, watching for any customer who may park on the lot or at the curb. The raised platform of the showroom gives us a very good line of sight.

Another reason it's higher is the psychological effect it has on you. You park and walk *up* to the showroom, not into it. By the time you're inside, you subconsciously feel that you are entering the dealer's kingdom. And because the rise in elevation is so subtle, you're not aware that you're feeling that. But you are. I know this and will use it to my advantage.

A raised showroom will also attract your eyes as you drive by. First, you're hooked on the front line display. Then your eyes naturally drift upward to the showroom. There you see brilliantly shining new cars in all their glory, basking in their shrine. And because the lighting is set to enhance that image, it could entice you to stop in and take a look. One more reason for the showroom to be higher than the lot has to do with test drives. While you're driving a new car, I'm trained to remain quiet until we're headed back to the lot. Then I'll ask a few questions as you park in front of the showroom. By being at a slight uphill angle, it entices you to feel as if this is where the battle begins. You're about to face down your enemy: me! If you get the car you want at the price you want, you'll become King of the Hill. That's exactly what I want you to think because I know all the tricks of the trade on how to sell you. I'll beat you, yet I'll let you leave thinking you're the winner!

THE TYPES OF CUSTOMERS
WHO WILL GET SCREWED

You may do many things wrong right from the start. You might be arrogant, distant, or insulting. Don't act this way. Be educated and friendly. Be interested in the product, but don't drool over it. And most importantly, BE HONEST. Even if I'm not.

Respectable salespeople appreciate honesty. In return, they'll treat you well. As for the shyster, schlock salesperson, honesty is one thing he doesn't know how to deal with. He has no come-back, technique, or psychology to combat it. All his training and work practices have been built on the lying customer. There's an old saying in the car business, "How can you tell a customer is lying? His lips are moving!"

Be honest. You'll never gain the upper hand with it if you deal with a blue-suede-shoes salesperson, but you can level the playing field a bit more in your favor. On the other hand, if you're fortunate enough to work with an honorable salesperson, your honesty could make a big impression. Honesty will get you the respect of the professional consultant.

One of the worst things you can do is walk onto the lot with a chip on your shoulder, telling me you've done your research online and you know exactly how much we paid for our cars. The same goes for telling me you have a relative or friend in the business and you're aware of all the sales tactics we use on customers. What you've done is immediately divulged your game plan. That sets me into motion. I know immediately what kind of customer you are. I know exactly how to play you and find your weak spot. I'll watch your body language and facial expressions. Eventually, I'll either catch you in a lie or find your vulnerability and exploit it.

If you have inside knowledge, especially from this book, DON'T EVER TELL THE SALESPERSON THAT! Keep it to yourself and use it for leverage when negotiating. Maybe you have someone with you and you're showing off. Or you may be alone and think you know how to play the game. You believe that in no way will I ever make you take a test drive or get figures if you don't want to. No way will you let me show you a green GT when you want a blue one with black interior. You'll only look at the car you want to buy. Guess what? I've been trained for over 30 years on how to overcome objections from pigeons. And I put it to work at least five times a day!

On the average, I saw about five customers every weekday, eight on Saturday, and six on Sunday. That comes out to an average of 34 customers per week, or 240 per month, about 2,800 customers per year.

That makes 14,000 customers in a five-year period. You buy a new car maybe once every five years. As a pro salesman, I get to hone my craft 14,000 times by the time you show up on the lot. I've had 14,000 opportunities to polish the psychology of selling. I know how to overcome objections and how to get the most money from you.

You, more than likely, have bought three cars or fewer in the past ten years. I've negotiated about 28,000 times! So who always has the upper hand when it comes to negotiations? Not you. Check your ego at the door. And if you find mine offensive, turn around and walk out without glancing back. Don't turn around for any reason. I don't deserve your business.

Keeping your distance because you want me to work for a sale is another technique that will backfire on you. It's a silly game. You come on the lot and act like you have no interest at all in our cars. You tell me very little as to what you're looking for and your time frame for purchasing. You want me to beg you to divulge this information. You think that will put you in control of the sale. In actuality, what that does is make me walk away from you and not give you the time of day.

You're interested in a certain model and you have questions about it—that's why you're here. But you won't get any answers from me, not with that attitude. You're wasting my time, as well as your own. Leave the head games to children. If you want to know more about a certain model, ask me. In fact, if all you want is information, tell me up front. Ask for a brochure and my card. Honesty, remember? I've got no comeback for that. And you've made no commitment. Getting my card does not mean you have to set an appointment with me.

The third type of customer starts off by degrading our cars. The mindset here is the more you attack our product, the more I'll bend over to get your business. At least, that's what you think. Guess again. I'll counter by asking you what you do for a living. Then I'll verbally assault your product or business. I've made my point. And I don't care if you leave because you're the type of person who will nit-pick your new car to death and never give me a moment's peace once you buy it.

One other personality we hate to see on the lot is the "second baseman." This is your neighbor, uncle, dad—whoever—that you bring in to negotiate for you. You're the one buying the car but this other person has a puffed up chest and is ready to show off his sales knowledge. Since this type of person is the most irritating to us, we cut him off right away. As soon as he starts spouting off about being wise to us, I'll turn to you and ask, "Who's buying the car?" You answer that you are. I look you straight in the eyes and say, "Then you're the one I'm talking to." I just cut him out of the picture. If he tries to negotiate again, I'll shake your hand and thank you for coming in, and then walk away.

Here's a tip if you have to bring in someone to negotiate for you: Make it plainly known that he is not to pull an attitude or get off on an ego trip. He's to remain friendly and business-like all the time. He's there to listen to you negotiate and help out only when he suspects you're being taken advantage of. If he speaks up, he'll do it in a conversational way. If he agrees to do that, you'll be surprised at how good a deal you can get mostly on your own. If he doesn't, you'll both be shown the door.

CHAPTER 15

Sizing You Up:
Types of Customers
and Their Personalities

How do you have a pleasant experience and get a fair deal in less than two hours—without fear, intimidation, or aggravation? You've laid out the groundwork so far with all your research and investigations. You know which dealers to visit and which to give a pass. You're aware of the type of personality you should have on the lot. The last piece of the puzzle is your salesperson.

You've just parked and you're walking onto the lot. I come up to greet you. I can be one of two types of salesmen. Do I greet you as you're getting out of the car? Or do I wait until you fully exit? If I'm the first type, beware. This is a warning sign that this may be a heavy pressure house. And I'm the typical schlock salesman. If I wait until you're completely out of the car, there's a very good chance I'll be a pleasant person to work with. (My personal method of selling had always been to let you walk on the lot and look over a few cars. I want you to have time to breathe and feel at ease before I greet you.)

When I approach you, am I walking at a quick pace, as if I'm ready to pounce on you? Or do I stroll up to you and smile? When I introduce myself, do I rush my hand out to you? Or do I casually bring it up to you? Do I ask you what you're interested in right away? Or do I first welcome you to the dealership? In all these instances, the second type is the most preferred. If I do any of the first approaches, I'm clueing you in as to what you're in store for. This is the nightmare most of you experience and this is why buying a car can cause grief, regret, and tremendous stress.

If I walk aggressively up to you, throw my hand at you, and ask what model you want to see, before I even introduce myself, you need to tell me you're not in the market for at least six months, if not more. And hold firm. Don't listen to any of the suggestions I give you for buying now. Completely tune me out. Make me walk away. Or better still, you leave and buy your car elsewhere. I don't deserve your business.

The blue-suede-shoes salesperson may take the time to introduce himself but then will immediately follow up with, "Are you buying today?" Or, "What car can I show you?" The first question is outright rude and a hustle. The second question is just as bad but without sounding that way. If you answer the second question with a definite make or model, the dollar signs in my eyes light up! I know right from the start that you have a certain car in mind. That means an easier road to making a sale. All I have to do is find the car on the lot, get you to drive it, and you'll fall in love with it. Before you know it, you're in the finance office signing a contract. No, the figures aren't exactly what you were hoping for. But so what? You've already got yourself hooked and you can't wait to drive it home and show it off. And I can't wait to see the commission I made off you. Your emotional attachment to a new car will always betray you.

So how do we size you up? The first thing we do is pre-judge you. Are you a real customer, or just a tire kicker? Do you look credit-worthy? Upside-down in the trade you just drove up in? Are you with your family? Do you have a "second baseman" with you to get you a deal? These are the ways we evaluate you before we even say "hi" to you! We immediately look for these signs:

1. How many people are with you.

2. The type of attire.

3. The gait at which you walk onto the lot.

4. The type of car you pull up in.

5. The license plate frames on your car.

In my experience, family people are more apt to buy a car now. A husband and wife are strong potential buyers. A husband and wife with kids are almost a sure bet. A gay couple will probably purchase, with a little bit of haggling. A lesbian couple may do a lot of haggling and a 50–50 chance of buying. A son or daughter with a dad is also a 50–50 proposition. A son or daughter with a mom is less than that. A 30-something female with a much older male is a sure sign he's a "second baseman", a friend who is there to make sure the female doesn't get taken. Most times, the second baseman will talk his friend out of a decent deal by throwing ego and attitude at me.

None of this is meant to stereotype or insult anyone. This is just the way it truly is. This information is strictly to help you realize the difference in treatment you may get if you are any one of these "types." If you are, knowledge is power. Knowing how to avoid being typecast by a salesperson will benefit you.

Next, we watch the way you walk onto the lot. A swagger means you've got an ego you want to throw around. A slow pace means you're just a tire kicker. A regular pace is a very good sign that you're in the market. Staring into the showroom or at the sales staff as you walk up is a good bet you're fearful and on the defensive right from the start. The same goes for walking up and avoiding any eye contact with the staff. Walking too fast can mean either a very eager customer or a looky-loo who just wants to test drive a car.

What kind of clothes are you wearing? Depending on the type of car I sell, that will dictate the proper apparel for you. Over-dressed for our lot? That's a YELLOW FLAG. I must approach with caution. It could mean you just got off your office job. Or you have credit problems that you hope we'll overlook because your expensive clothes say that's all in the past. You can afford major purchases now. Yeah, right. Think again!

Underdressed? A RED FLAG. It could mean you're simply very casual and leisurely, and therefore not a serious buyer. Or it could be you're looking at cars your credit or finances can't afford. But once in awhile, you'll be underdressed intentionally so that we'll leave you alone and let you browse at your leisure.

Driving a car less than a year old? It's a very good chance it's not a trade-in. One to two years old? You're upside-down in it. You owe more than what it's worth. Three to four years old? A 50–50 chance you have equity.

What about the license plate frames? What dealer did this car come from? Certain dealers in every town are notorious for burying their customers in car payments. I know which ones they are. So does every salesperson that stays informed on his competition.

By putting the age of your vehicle together with where it came from, I can jump to an immediate conclusion as to your ability to buy a new car. Next, I need to quickly establish the relationship between you and the people you've brought with you. Are you a male/female couple without kids? I have to find out if the female is the buyer. Is the male your spouse or significant other, or a "second baseman" who wants to prevent you from getting ripped off?

As I mentioned earlier, a male aged 50 or more who comes in with a 30-something female is a sure sign of a second baseman—with one notable exception. If the older man is a good neighbor and you're a single mom, he's there for the same reason as the egotistical second baseman— to help you negotiate—but he tends to listen more and be more rational. No matter how much of a schlock salesman I am, I can't help but respect him for what he's doing and I tend to deal more realistically with him.

Only in rare cases does this type of couple happen to be spouses or a father and daughter. The father buying a car for his daughter always comes alone the first time. He wants to size up the dealer and sales staff. He finds a salesperson he feels comfortable with, and checks out a few cars his daughter may like. Then he brings her to the dealership the next day.

Okay, I've just sized you up before we've even met. Now I need to ask key questions that will clue me into the type of personality you are. By finding this out at the start, I'll have a clear idea how to handle you and any objections you may have. Car buyers usually exhibit one of four personality types:

- Analytical
- Dominant
- Solid
- Expressive

If you're analytical, you'll have a cold, flat voice with little inflection. You'll want to know why things are arranged the way they are on the car. You'll ask how my car compares with that of our competition. When it comes to the write-up, you'll want me to explain step by step what I'm doing and how I arrived at that figure. You want brief and to-the-point answers. No superfluous responses.

If you're dominant, you'll want to control the conversation. You'll want to decide when I can show you a car. You will ask me a question about the car, and before I finish answering, you'll ask another question. You'll look over the car in the order you want, not in the order I want to present it. You'll test drive only if you want to, and you'll most likely take the route you want to drive. At the write-up, you'll want our best price quickly, and then take your time thinking it over.

If you're solid, you're very structured in what you want: a basic cake with very little frosting. It's the way you've always eaten it, and the way you always will. Same with the type of car you want to buy. (We don't bother showing the solid type anything but exactly what she wants because it'll be a waste of her time.) You don't like to talk much. You'd rather be shown a car and be able to take it in without a lot of chatter from me. You know exactly what you want and nothing else will do.

If you're expressive, you're very outgoing, friendly, and love to talk shop about the car you're interested in. You're eager to learn everything you can about the car, as well as tell me facts and anecdotes that you know about it. You'll enjoy the test drive. You'll spend a lot of time shooting the breeze. And you're the most inclined to buy right now.

By sizing you up as a certain type of customer, I'll know if I should spend time with you or move on to someone else. If I feel you are a potential buyer, by learning your personality quickly, I'll know the right approach to take with you. This puts me a step ahead.

So you thought selling cars was easy? All it took was a loud-mouth, balding, fat guy, in a loud plaid suit, with an obnoxious personality? I wish! Selling cars and being good at it means being a carnival barker, a chameleon, a psychiatrist, and an encyclopedia on what we sell. It takes years to learn and perfect the craft. Fortunately for you, you're learning it quickly—from this book.

CHAPTER 16

Nightmare on Auto Mall Street

Of all the signs that tell you to walk off a car lot immediately, the most glaringly obvious is the blue-suede-shoes guy. As I've mentioned before, he is the person who will say anything and do anything to make the sale. To better illustrate, I'm going to use dialogue. The scene: you casually walk onto the lot. I rush up to you with my arm already extended for a handshake and a greedy grin on my face.

> ME: *Hi! What brings you to Shady Sam's Motors?* (I didn't even tell you my name or ask for yours.)
>
> YOU: *I'm looking for a GT coupe.*
>
> ME: *GT coupe? You really know your cars.* (I'm stroking your ego.) *They're a hot seller.* (I'm setting you up to pay more than you wanted.) *We only have two left.* (I'm creating an urgency to buy now.)
>
> YOU: *Have you got a blue one with black interior?*
>
> ME: *Take a look at this: green with tan leather!* (I'm not listening to you at all.)
>
> I open the door, wave you into the car. You refuse.
>
> YOU: *I'm just looking.*

ME: *And I'm just showing.* (It's the perfect comeback. You can't say anything to that.)

YOU: *Uh . . . I'm not in the market right now. I'm just killing time.*

ME: *We had six last week. We're down to two.* (I'm reinforcing the urgency to buy now.)

I wait a moment to see if you walk away. You don't. Now I fish around to see if you bite.

ME: *Go ahead. Sit in it. You came all this way.* (I'm overcoming your objections by making you feel obligated to sit.)

YOU: *Well, Okay. But I only have a few minutes to kill. I have a doctor's appointment.*

Now I know you're lying. Would you go out of your way just to look or kill time at a grocery store—especially if you had an appointment in five minutes across town? No way. You go to a market for a reason—to buy groceries. You go to a car lot for a reason—to buy a car. The excuses range from picking up your spouse or kids to meeting someone for lunch or dinner. Whatever you use, I know it's a lie. And that gives me a blank check to say and do anything to keep you there until you buy. So I start by throwing your lie right back at you.

ME: *Me too. I have an appointment coming in, in a few minutes.* (How does it feel to be lied to?)

You sit in the driver's seat. I close the door. By closing it, I'm subconsciously showing you I'm in control. I'm calling the shots. Now I sit in the passenger's seat and begin the presentation to make you get an emotional attachment to it. Once you do, I'm halfway home to a sale! I show you the faux carbon fiber trim. I have you run your hand over it. I make you grip the steering wheel and grab the shifter. I want you to imagine you're actually driving the car.

Once you smile or nod your head, I turn the key and fire it up. I do a judgment call by asking you questions in a certain way. Then I carefully listen to how you answer. If you use the same phrasing I used in my questions when answering, I know I've got you right where I want you.

ME: *How's that sound?*

YOU: *Sounds great. I love the V-8 rumble.*

ME: *What'd you think of the horsepower?*

YOU: *I love the horsepower. The way it takes off from a dead stop.*

Bingo! I've got a live one. I stay quiet for a minute while I watch you make a connection to the car. Then I stroke your ego again, making you want to take it out for a test drive.

ME: *You've done a lot of research on this car. I don't need to tell you about how fast it is or how it handles.* (A statement specifically made to get you to talk up the car.)

YOU: *Yeah. It's really impressive. This car can really haul. And it can out-handle anything in its class.*

CHA-CHING! Emotional connection plus parroting me! These are the cues I've been waiting for. But I need to play it up as if I shouldn't take you out on the pavement. That will make you want to drive it even more. I've got to build up your emotional attachment to its peak.

ME: *I'd let you drive it but I've got that appointment coming in any moment.* (I pause. You're let down.) *But I guess it'll be all right to take it around the block.*

Your eyes light up. I ask for your driver's license to make a copy of it. It's standard procedure for a test drive. In case you get in an accident, our dealer insurance will cover our liability as long as you had permission to drive it. I look it over and ask you if all the information is current. If it is, I have what I need for the write-up afterwards. If it isn't current, I still continue on. Next, I ask for your phone number. I ask in a friendly way so as not to induce any fear in you. After all, I'm putting my "appointment" aside for you. I'm a nice guy, right?

We take the GT out on the street. I'm already planning my trial close on you. I tell you the route we commonly use. But we'll have to cut it short. By saying this, I'm setting you up for my "good guy" act. And getting you closer to a sale.

ME: *This is where we should turn back—but you know what? Go a little further.*

I'm now your friend. Not a car salesman. You grin. I wait for a moment, and then I hit you up with an irresistible offer.

ME: *To hell with it. Let's go the full distance.*

Now I'm a great guy, on your side. And you feel confident that you'll get a fair deal because we're friends. You ask me the price of the car. I NEVER talk price until we're back at my desk, doing a write-up. I show you more features the car has to deflect your question. And inside I am elated because I'm thinking about how close I am to making a huge commission! You drive back to the dealership.

ME: *Now what do you think of its performance? Is it everything you thought it would be?* (I call this the trial close question.)

YOU: *It's even better than I thought.*

You pull back up on the lot. My "appointment" is forgotten now. So is yours! You ask about the price again as we get out. I show you the MSRP. You wince. I mention it's only the suggested price. You want to see what I can do for you, since we're on the same wave length—or so you think. Your emotional attachment is at its peak. You've even forgotten you came in looking for a blue GT.

We go inside the showroom to my desk. You start to get cold feet. You're still a bit reluctant to make the commitment. But I have so many ways to get around that. The fact that you did everything I told you to do leaves me in full control. I got you to drive the car and to fall in love with it. You have already closed yourself with your emotional attachment to it. All I need to do is nudge you to sign on the dotted line.

Whether you're a 40-year-old businessman, a single mom with two kids, or a 60-year-old grandparent—whatever your situation is—I'll customize my delivery to build up your desire to buy a car, and to correspond with your personality type. I'll work every angle I have to get you to make that emotional commitment. And I did that very successfully for almost 30 years. Welcome to Shady Sam Motors!

CHAPTER 17

The Write-Up

The most common write-up sheet is called a "four square." It's a standard 8″ × 11″ sheet of paper divided into four sections. First I fill in the top lines with your name and address. I get that information from the copy of your driver's license. If it isn't correct, without missing a beat, I ask you for your current information, which you gladly disclose. Then I fill in your phone number.

Square one is where I write the stock number and type of car you just drove. Major options are also hand-written in this square. That's to reinforce the "I gotta have it" feeling you're currently reeling in.

The second square has the list price of the car. There's enough room in this square for "first pencil" and further negotiations. First pencil is a term used by sales managers and closers. It's commonly used in a high-pressure straight-sell or turn-over house. It works this way: I write in the list price. You tell me what you want to pay for it. I take that price to "the desk." If it's a straight-sell dealer, the sales manager will write in a higher counter offer, or "first pencil." The hard sell negotiations begin. If it's a turn-over house, the closer comes to you with the four square in hand and starts hammering away at you. But before that happens, he tells me to go back and to fill in the other two boxes. Then he'll sit down in front of you and give you his verbal first pencil, which can get very ugly.

The third square is the monthly payment. You can easily get hammered here because I play the "up-sell" game. I ask you what kind of payment you're looking for.

YOU: *$400 a month.*

ME: *Up to?*

YOU: *Up to $450 a month.*

ME: *Okay, so you can afford $450 if you need to?*

YOU: *Yeah. But I don't want to pay that much.*

I nod. I don't verbally reply because I don't want to promise you anything. Why not? Because you just bumped yourself another $50 a month in less than two seconds! And I'm going to take as much of that as I can. A nod is not implying any commitment on my side.

See how easy it is for me to get you to set yourself up? I've manipulated you from the moment I opened the door to the GT and got you to sit in it. And now I'm really going to work on you.

At this point, you feel a little bit uncomfortable but you still believe I'm a great guy and will get you a deal you can't pass up. So you sit still in your chair and let me "put you together" in the car.

Square four is the trade-in information. I write in the year, make, and model. Then I take an appraisal sheet and ask you for your keys and registration. If I detect hesitation from you, I assure you it's only so the used car manager can drive it around the block to see if everything works. We also need to be sure your registration is current and that it has no liens on it. I put you at ease.

We both go out to your car. I do a walk-around and you follow me. Without saying a word, I rub the dings and scratches. I notice the pits in the windshield. Fade spots in the paint. You're starting to sweat. Not only have I caught all the impurities of your car, you don't know for sure what I'm thinking since I remain silent. But you think it can't be very good.

Now I check the tires and the interior. I make all the notes on my appraisal sheet, smile at you, and tell you we'll go back inside so I can give this to my manager. If you ask what I'm doing, I'll just say I'm making my manager's job easier by giving him all this information. And then I drop the subject. I let my silence create fearful anxiety in you. After all, I'm a blue-suede-shoes salesperson. I want you to sweat so that even though you don't like our appraisal, you'll still take it because we found all those problems with your car. This is known as beating down the value. To be sure, your trade-in is not worth close to what you think it is. But that doesn't mean we have carte blanch to steal it from you.

All right, so now we have all four boxes filled in. I take this write-up sheet to my manager or closer. He looks over the payment info to be sure I set you up right. Then he draws a line through your figure of what you want to pay and writes in a higher figure, giving him enough room to haggle. First pencil is a clever way to gauge just how eager you are for the car. The closer or I will closely watch your facial expression and body language as the counter offer is presented to you. The more eager you are to haggle and become a buyer, the higher our commission will be.

The last bit of paperwork is the credit application. A shyster will put that in front of you before the actual write-up begins. He claims he needs to know what interest rate he can get you and this will help him give you accurate numbers. What he's actually doing is gauging how badly you want the car. The easier you fill it out, the more commission he's counting on.

Most salespeople will wait until the four boxes are filled out to pull out the application. The reasoning behind this is that I've shown you what a great guy I am and I've taken the time to go step by step through the four square form with you. No pressure. Your guard is down. Now comes the time to really press hard for a commitment.

I'm watching your body language and "taking your temperature." By getting you to fill out the application now, I'm almost home with another sale. If you refuse at this point, I have a great way to counter that. I tell you I'll try to get your payment where you want it. But by not having all the information I need, I can't promise it. I do a song and dance in the sales manager or closer's office, depending on if it's a straight-sell or turn-over house. I tell him about the "appointment" ruse.

The closer or manager comes out, shakes your hand, and sits down. Now the double talk and pressure reaches its peak. He tells you we're just shooting at the moon without knowing your credit score. You don't budge. He emphasizes how my appointment came in while we were on the road. He doesn't say any more than that. (Of course not, since there was no appointment!) The idea is to build up guilt in you—let you jump to the conclusion that I missed out on a sale.

YOU: *I wanted a blue GT with black leather. Not green with tan leather.*

HIM: *Blue is a very popular color. That makes it hard to find. But I'm sure you know that. You've already done your shopping.* (Naturally, you'll agree. You want to appear knowledgeable, a psychological ploy to take your defenses away.)

ME: I *sold a blue one over the weekend at sticker.*

He looks directly at me, feigning disgust.

HIM: *It shoulda gone for a grand over 'cuz it's so hot.*

Now he turns to you.

HIM: *He* (referring to me) *wanted to take the guy's offer of $500 off. I said, "Are you serious? It's our last one and there aren't any others around!"*

Now he's set you up to accept two things:

1. Taking the green GT.
2. Taking any discount you're offered.

By leaving his statement open or unfinished, he's leaving it to you, once again, to jump to conclusions. Then he plays our trump card to be sure you'll take the green one.

HIM: *And you know what? Three or four years down the road when they want to trade in their blue GTs, they'll get a lot less for them because the market is flooded with them. So they take a beating when they buy it at sticker. And they take another beating when they trade it in. Doesn't make sense, does it?*

That last question is rhetorical. He is merely cementing you into the green one with that. We both know you'll agree that it's stupid to take a hit twice on one car. So you just sold yourself a green GT when you really wanted blue. You've got nowhere to go from there.

This brings up the subject of how we hook you to commit to buying. After all the boxes are filled in on the four square and you do a credit application, I cross out the closer's, or manager's number and write in a price about $250 less. I have you to sign the write-up sheet that states you will buy the GT at this specific price. I tell you it's not a binding contract—which it truly isn't. Then I ask you to write a check for $2,500 to show how serious you are. I convince you that with this, I now have leverage to try to get that price. And I give you an out. If I can't get the car at this price, I'll give you your check back. I have to by California law. Check your local laws just to be sure. Well, even my additional $250 discount price gives me a pretty good commission and I know it's a done deal.

You write the check. I take that and the four square with your credit application into the manager's office so he can pat me on the back for a job well done. Then he puts his signature on it and it's off to the finance department. But if you still haven't filled out the credit application and are waiting until you find out what the final selling price is, I go into the manager's office and another ploy goes into gear. He comes out and it's show time! He says he'll agree to the lower price and will do his best to get you the interest rate you want but he needs to see if you qualify.

We finally run your credit and, sure enough, you won't qualify for Tier A. Even if you have outstanding credit. But my manager "can get you the next best rate." That's when he shows you your credit report. We know what everything on it means. The credit score, the category results, the codes. You know only your FICO score. So he'll fast-talk his explanation of why, even though you have a 720 FICO, you're not Tier A. And you'll buy his story. If you ask for your check back, he'll give you the "good guy" routine:

> MANAGER/CLOSER: *I know you have a really good rapport with (my name) and he's tried very hard to work for you. I don't want to see you leave without the car so here's what I'll do: Let's get the contract signed at the Tier B rate and I'll do everything I can tomorrow to get you a better rate. I'll personally call the finance company and go to bat for you. And if I can get you a better deal, we'll rewrite the contract at the lower price. It has happened before. (That's the tease to give you hope that it may happen for you.)*

You agree. I congratulate you on your purchase and reassure you that I'll make sure my manager calls first thing tomorrow. You sign the contracts. The car is now yours. You drive the GT off the lot.

After you leave, I get with the sales manager. We plan our next move. Tier A credit is 3.9% interest. Tier B is 6.9%. We wrote you up at Tier B knowing that you were strong enough for Tier A. Why? Because we then go into our next phase. I call you the next day. I tell you to bring your contract back. We're going to rewrite it at a lower rate. That puts you in a happy mood. It erases any buyer's remorse you may now feel. We know that you'll greatly appreciate any reduction in interest. And we'll still make money off you.

You arrive and I immediately take you into the sales manager's office. He says it was tough but he really went to bat for you. It took some crunching but he finally got them to agree to a 5.35% rate. Then he shows you how much you'll save every month. Right now, you'll shine our shoes and clean our offices. You're so happy about the savings and how much we did for you. We just made an additional 1.45% off you. We bumped you that much without blinking an eye. And you can't thank me enough!

This is not the only way to play this game. It's got many variations. It all depends on your age and gender and personality type. If you're a male in your 20s wanting a V-8 GT, or a young or mid-age female wanting a safe car, this ploy works best. If you're a mid-age male or parents wanting a family car, we'll hit you high on the rate. Then the sales manager says he'll send it in *immediately* to the finance company to see if he can get a better rate. Of course he can. That's part of our plan. And it's how we get you to bite at the lower rate that is still higher than what you actually qualify for. Buyers age 60 and older usually pay cash. On the chance they do finance, we'll use the sincerity approach and mention our own parents. We want that connection with you so when we give you a rate, it sounds trustworthy to you.

If you're the type who brags about knowing how to buy a car and we can't pull anything over on you, we have an approach for that too. We call your bluff. We bring the finance manager in on it. You're fixated on the interest rate. I give you an estimate. My sales manager has already called the finance manager and told him what number to hit you up with and why. The finance manager gets the contract printed out and calls us into his office. You ask him for the interest rate. He tells you he'll get to that. First he wants to go over all the numbers with you on the contract. He hears you're a very smart buyer and wants to make sure you know everything up front. What an ego stroke!

He matter-of-factly tells you the retail and selling price of your vehicle, tax, license and documentation fee, your trade-in value, the total cost of the car, how many months the contract is for, and the interest rate. And he emphasizes that it's based on your credit score and history. Without missing a beat, he continues on with all disclosures that are required by the state. And there are many of them. He gets to the end and asks you if you understand everything that he explained. It's a lot of information.

You want to keep up the impression that you are a wise buyer so you nod. And you don't mention the interest rate again. That would be an admission on your part that you don't understand everything on the contract after all. If you do ask about the interest rate, he'll tell you once again, very matter-of-factly. Then, still without missing a beat, he'll hand you a pen and have you start signing the contract and disclosures. If you balk again, he'll tell you that if you think you can do better, go ahead. But he can't guarantee the car will be available when you come back. We just sold _____ of these cars over the weekend and are now down to just _____.

What if you tell us that your credit union or bank can do better? Great! We'll make it an Option Contract. You have five days to bring us a check to cover the car from your credit union or bank and we'll tear up our contract. If not, we'll send this one in. Chances are in our favor that you won't have a check for us.

And if you do, well, we tried. I must repeat once again that your attitude at a dealership can bury you in finance. Our pens are mightier than swords. If you're being difficult, we'll have you sign the contract, then play the "call the bank in the morning to see if we can get a better rate" game on you. And when I do call you tomorrow, it's to tell you that we tried really hard but couldn't do much better. Why couldn't we? Simple: You had an attitude!

So there you have it: the worst type of selling techniques. Dealers use other variations but they're still similar in style and outcome. Now you know what we do, why we do it, and how we hook you and reel you in. A real pro can talk you into anything. The more you drop our sales lingo into the conversation, or the more you emphasize that you're wise to us, the better our prospects are to make a very good commission off you. We're trained in all the different types of customers and how to counter your objections. We know how to challenge you when you claim to be onto us.

I'll wrap up this chapter with a quick rundown of all the things that went wrong for you in this situation:

1. I aggressively approached you and you waited for me.
2. You gave away your game plan by letting me know that you were wise to us.
3. I didn't listen to you at all. You wanted a blue GT. I pushed you into a green one.
4. I got you to make an emotional connection with the green one during the test drive.
5. I countered all your objections with non-committal nods and "mmm-hmmms," or by changing the subject.
6. I made sure your emotional connection never waned.
7. My closer went to work on you on the price of the car.
8. My sales manager and finance manager played you on the interest rate.

All these things added up to my controlling the sale all the way through. By telling me right at the start that you know how to play the game, or by answering my specifically designed questions, you gave away any hope of getting a good deal. Now that you really know how we work, never let on. Keep this to yourself. Never give away your battle plans. You should've walked away as soon as I greeted you aggressively. Or at the very least, when I didn't listen to you. Bottom line: my closer, sales manager, finance manager, and I made a very nice commission off you!

CHAPTER 18

Your Trade-In

As I mentioned before, your trade is not worth anywhere near what you think it is. It's a common mistake everybody makes—including salespeople! We trade in our cars just like you. I have argued with the used car manager, who's a friend, about my car's true value.

We get attached to our cars, even when they're giving us so much trouble that we have to trade them in. But the truth is your car is NOT in absolute pristine condition. It's not going to bring you as much as you think. Pristine means it looks as perfectly new as the day you drove it off the lot. But that isn't the way your car looks. Just getting it washed, even at a brushless carwash, will put surface scratches in the paint. And how long has it been since you had the interior completely detailed? Probably never. Is the engine bay clean enough to eat off of? Very doubtful. I won't even ask about the undercarriage.

Save yourself a lot of shock, anger and indigestion. Before you go to the dealerships to shop, find every fault in your trade-in. Start by having your car washed and waxed. Have the interior and under the hood cleaned. And by all means, clean out the trunk! This means vacuuming it if necessary and putting the spare tire and jack in its proper place.

Park it in the sun. Now do a walk around with a very cynical eye. Check for every imperfection you can find. Be super-critical. Put yourself in the used car manager's shoes. Try to find anything you can use to knock down the price of your trade-in. Inspect the paint. Do you see pits and scratches? How many dings can you find? What about dents? Are your wheels or wheel covers chipped? Do they have curb rash? Examine the windshield. Rub your fingers gently over it. Do you feel all those pits? What about holes or cracks? How about the exterior moldings? Are any peeling off? Are any dented? How much tread is left on your tires? Does the car have body rust?

Under the hood, does the car look road-worthy, or should the vacuum and water hoses be replaced? What about the fuel lines? Are any mechanical repairs needed that can be seen by the naked eye? How much oil is leaking around the valve covers and manifolds? How much oil drips on the ground? Transmission fluid leaks? Creaks in the suspension?

Now check the interior. Do the seats have worn spots? How about the carpet and floor mats? Is the headliner tearing or pulling away? Is the dash pad or steering wheel cracked? Are there indelible stains anywhere in the interior? Are the door panels warped or falling apart? How about the sun visors?

Turn on the ignition. Do you hear strange or loud noises at start-up? How about at idle? Do you feel a vibration? Try all the electrical accessories. Do they work well without straining? Does your tilt wheel bind? Is the inside rear view mirror glued on tightly? Does the radio/CD player work properly? How about the illuminated vanity mirrors?

Now go for a drive with the radio off and windows up. Check the air conditioner and heater. Do they work well? Shut them off and listen for any noises as you accelerate or brake. Does the car hesitate when you accelerate? Does it shudder when you brake? Does the cruise control work? Does the transmission shift smoothly?

Turn hard left, then right. Do you hear a grinding sound? Does the steering wheel lock up on hard turns? Go over a couple dips and bumps. Does the suspension make clunking or grinding sounds? Does the car bounce more than twice? Does it bottom out? A used car manager will search your car for all these things. He does all this in the few minutes he's with your car. You'll probably need at least a half hour to cover everything.

Be very critical. Find everything wrong with your car before you shop. Then you'll have a better understanding why you weren't offered as much as you first believed it was worth. But if you have your car detailed inside out and cleaned under the hood and the trunk too, you may find that this will increase the value of your car a little bit. It will have eye appeal—that is, if you don't have any serious interior or exterior damage.

WHAT A DEALER DOES WITH YOUR TRADE-IN

A dealer does one of three things with your old car:

1. Reconditions and re-sells it.
2. Wholesales it off because it needs too many repairs, has excessive mileage, or is not a car the dealer can sell.
3. Sells it as-is to an employee.

If a car is too old, needs too much work, or the mileage is too high, the dealer will call a few wholesalers for a price. Wholesalers own used car lots and need lower-priced cars to sell.

If it's an exotic, like a Porsche, or a specialty, like an Audi RS-4, the used car manager will call those specific dealers for a price and sell it to the highest bidder since he can't successfully re-sell that car on his lot.

On the other hand, if your car is a Taurus or Camry, for example, and you buy a new Mercedes E 420, that dealer will most likely sell your trade to the highest bidder of that brand, since it's not something he'd want on his lot. But it's a car a Ford or Toyota dealer would want.

Sometimes an employee sees a trade-in that he knows is a wholesale piece. He wants it. The used car manager will buy your trade-in and resell it, as-is, to the employee, without any guarantees, expressed or implied. The employee doesn't mind. He can fix it at a minimal cost to make it road-worthy since he works there.

In most, if not all states, every used car must be clearly marked with a buyer's guide that specifies whether this car has a limited warranty or is sold as-is. A tremendous liability issue is involved. If your car is one the dealer wants to sell with either a limited warranty or a Certified Warranty, then a lot of reconditioning will go into your trade-in. The dealer must go through the engine, transmission, brakes, rear end, suspension, door glass, and windshield, and repair anything that will prevent the car from running smoothly or safely. If any major repairs are needed, such as the air conditioner or air bags, they must be fixed.

Next, it has to pass a safety and smog inspection. After that, any accessories that are not working right, such as a power window or the radio, must be repaired. Then it has to be completely detailed, inside and out—which is why, if you do it ahead of trading it in, you may end up with a bit more than if you hadn't. Of course, some cosmetic things don't get repaired or replaced since they don't prevent the car from being road worthy. But you'll still get dinged for them when you trade it in!

TO TRADE OR NOT TO TRADE

The answer is YES, trade it in! Save yourself a lot of unnecessary grief, aggravation, and time. Sure, you can always get more selling it yourself. But stop and think of what that involves. The most important factor is your safety. Do you want strangers coming to your door and driving your car? In today's world, that is not an ideal situation. Don't forget, you have to advertise your car, which can cost anywhere from $40 to $150—even more if it doesn't sell in the first week.

You have to take calls at all hours of the day and set up appointments. Most of the callers never show up so you waste a lot of time waiting. The few who do show up are going to tear your car apart and lowball you on your price. I find it ironic that the one type of salesman everyone despises—the schlock talker—is exactly what they become when they look over a private party car for sale!

If you're lucky enough to find a buyer, you have to go to their bank first to withdraw funds. Then it's over to your bank to deposit them. Once again, safety is involved here. Whether it's in cash or a bank check, you're in possession of a lot of money that can easily be taken from you.

Once you finish with the banks, it's off to the DMV for the registration and transfer of ownership paperwork. You want to be sure that you are no longer responsible for your former car and that the state knows this. This can take two to five hours of your time.

Another factor to consider is that, today, most people prefer to buy a used car at a new car dealership. They know that buying a private party car is buying someone else's headaches. They know that the car needs some repairs but they don't know how much they'll cost. They don't know the history of the car or its overall condition. But by buying at a dealership, they're getting a car that has been thoroughly reconditioned and has had a safety inspection. The car must have any recalls performed before it's resold.

It may also carry a limited warranty or a Certified Warranty, if it's not sold as-is. That's something you can't personally offer with your car. Even a high-pressure turn-over house will recondition its cars. Why? Because there's just too much liability involved if a newly purchased used car breaks down—or worse, the new owner is injured due to a safety related issue.

Liability also affects you too if you sell your car outright. It doesn't matter if you correctly go through all the procedures at the bank and the DMV. If something safety-related happens to the new owner, you could be at fault whether you were aware of the problem or not. And if the car should break down soon afterwards, the headaches that the new owners will cause you is just not worth it.

Trade it in and get it over with. Whatever additional money you could make selling it privately is not justified by the hell you'll go through if you try to sell it yourself. Turn your headache over to the dealer and let him handle it.

THE TRADE-IN BUMP

Some dealers will hold back about $500 on your trade-in value. They use it to sweeten your deal or put it into an account to use on somebody else. It works this way: The used car sales manager books out your car at $6,700. He says he'll give you $6,200. If you resist, he'll come back with another $50 more. Then $100, if he has to. He says he's "allowing," or "giving you an allowance" of the higher price to make the deal. On the contract you sign, it'll show the figure of $6,200 or more for your trade. But on the company ledger, he shows the full $6,700 at which he booked your car. The difference between what he gave you and what he shows on the ledger goes into his used car account to give "allowances" to others who balk at their appraisal.

Any dealer who will "allow" a higher figure for your trade-in, or give you an "allowance" on it is not to be trusted. He's not telling you the truth. The truth is Actual Cash Value. ACV is what your car is really worth. And an honest dealer will provide only that number, no other variations of it. You've already done your homework—the walk-around, then going online to get an estimate of your car's value. Now you're at the dealership and the used car manager gives you his figure. If it's in the ballpark of what you got online, you're in a good position.

TOO FAR APART

What if your figure and his are too far apart? Your best move would be to tell him you're not interested. Tell him you have to sell your car yourself before you can even think of buying a new one. Then stay silent. Wait for his next move. If he immediately bumps his offer higher by $300 or $400, there's a very good chance he's holding back a lot of cash. Not just the $500 that most do. That's why you are so far apart. This is not the kind of person you want to deal with. Get up and find another dealer who deserves your business.

Let's back up a step. The used car manager gives you a figure, say you want another $1000 and it's a deal. If he doesn't budge off his number, it means one of two things. Either you are the one who is way off on your appraisal, or he's really a blue-suede-shoes guy, right down to his heels. You need to find this out very quickly.

Have him show you how he arrived at that figure, step by step: first, the web site he used, and then the current auction reports on cars similar to yours. Auction reports tell him what cars like yours are currently going for "on the block." That's what a dealer must pay to buy a car just like yours to resell on his lot. It's the very best way to gauge your true trade-in value, or ACV. If he calmly shows you these and explains what the figures mean, he's giving you a real Actual Cash Value for your car. You can take his word that it truly is what your car is worth.

If he gives you grief or attitude, head for the door. Anyone who hides information from you is not being honest with you. He obviously doesn't want you to know how badly he's trying to screw you. And don't fall for a sigh. A used car manager will do that to make you think he has no more room to negotiate.

Maybe he really is at his limit. But you don't know for sure, so stay put and refuse to cave in and accept his last offer. Don't say another word. If he bumps himself up, you know the sigh was a ploy. If he doesn't you may have gotten the most you can for your trade-in.

Now, reiterate the price you agreed to pay for the new car, the price you agreed for your trade-in, and the finance rate at which you've been approved. Tell your salesman that you'll take the new car only if he locks in all those figures. You're just about ready to take delivery.

PROTECTING YOURSELF

Now let's assume that you and the used car sales manager are close in your figures on your trade-in. The next step is to refuse it. Tell him you want $500 more. If he stands pat, you did get the true value of your trade in. Take his offer. But if he bumps his figure, this starts the back-and-forth. You end up with $275 more than his original offer. Don't accept it just yet! Since he bumped himself that much you're aware that you didn't get the Actual Cash Value of your car. He gave you an allowance. This should make you very suspicious about getting a fair deal at this dealer. Stay Alert! You could get taken on the price of your new car or pay a higher rate in financing it.

The best way to protect yourself, if you don't trust the used car manager, is to ask him, "If I buy a new car somewhere else, will you still buy my car at the price you just gave me?" If you get any attitude, any hesitation, leave! Don't turn around or sit back down for any reason. They're trying to put you together. If he says no, but gives you a figure at which he will buy it, you now have something solid to work with. It's up to you to decide at this point if you want to move forward or try another dealer.

So, you see, there's a lot more going on when your car is appraised than you realized. It's time-consuming. It involves a physical inspection, a test drive, online research, making three calls to wholesalers or dealers of that brand, and presenting the price to you. Then it can take up to 30 minutes explaining to you why your car is not worth what you think it is.

Cut your trip to the dealership shorter than your last six-hour ordeal. Do your own walk-around, go online and use "Fair" or "Average" when pricing out your car. Add any hits to its value, such as accidents, mileage and excessive wear and tear. This will give you a very good dose of reality of your car's true worth.

CHAPTER 19

Financing Your Car, But Can't Get Approved?

As a car buyer, you have many ways to NOT get approved. One may be that your credit sucks! Or you have a very short credit report history, maybe just one or two years on file. Or you may have five or more years of credit history but it's all been with department store or gasoline credit cards. You have no major cards such as Visa or MasterCard. Or you are a first time buyer and want a car that costs too much.

Every manufacturer has a certain line of cars that you may qualify for if you are a first time buyer. For instance, you want a new GMC Yukon 4×4 SLT-2. That's a $50,000 SUV. That's not a vehicle for a first time buyer. The Chevrolet HHR is what you should be looking at. You'll have a lot better chance of getting approved on a $22,000 SUV than a full size, top-of-the-line vehicle.

What if you have the means to put $25,000 down on the Yukon? You still won't get approved. You have no car loan history established. You are too much of a risk. The finance company looks at the MSRP cost of the vehicle, not what you want to finance. They also look at the average insurance premium on that vehicle for your age and the cost of gas and maintenance too. It's just too much obligation for a first time buyer.

Most importantly, without any prior car buying history, the bank has no idea if you'll make all your payments—on time. What if you bought a lot of things on credit, such as a house, furniture, and a home theater system with a 64 inch plasma screen TV? But you always paid cash for your cars? That's a major negative on your credit report. Just like the first time buyer, you have never built up a car credit history with a lender. And now you're applying for a car loan?

Sure, you qualified for a $450,000 home loan and $40,000 worth of furnishings on credit but that doesn't matter. Getting approved on a house is a lot easier than on a car. A house cannot easily be moved or hidden. If you're delinquent on your mortgage payments and the bank forecloses, it will always know where to find the building it now owns. Home furnishings need a lot of space if you're going to store them. You have to rent commercial storage somewhere which is easily traceable. Everyone gets their products back. But a car is very mobile. It can be taken across a state border or stored in your garage. Or in a friend's garage. It may never be found. Without a history of car payments, you are a risk!

Do you have a lot of credit cards? You may think that the more you have with a low or no balance owed helps you. Wrong! Not if your annual income cannot justify the total amount of credit you have available from all your cards. Say you have ten credit cards. Your credit limit on all of them combined is $100,000. You carry a combined balance of $1,000, just 1% of debt-to-credit available. BUT—the lending institution for your auto loan will see that you make just $45,000 a year. You have the ability to spend an additional $99,000 on your cards, which you could never repay on your salary if you max them out. You're too much risk.

The optimum level of combined credit availability should be less than 34% of your annual income. The ideal number of credit cards you should have is four. Those cards must be in good standing without any 30-, 60-, or 90-day late pays. They should have 10% or less balance owed on them.

You should also have a prior auto loan history from a captive lending company, such as GMAC is to GM, or Honda Financial Services is to Honda. As with your credit cards, you should not have any late pays on it. Combine your rent or mortgage payment, car payment, personal loan and credit card payments. This is monthly debt-to-income ratio. This should not be more than 33% of your monthly income. Anything over that can hurt you or cause you to be turned down.

CHAPTER 20

The Four Tiers of Credit Ratings

Credit ratings come in four tiers: Tier A is the best, followed by Tier B, Tier C, and Tier D. Anything less than that is an automatic turn-down.

Tier A gets you the best interest rate. With each drop in ratings, your interest rate rises. If you want an incentivized rate, such as 1.9% interest at 60 months, you need to have Tier A credit. That's why you'll always hear a "__.__% interest available only to well qualified buyers" disclaimer on every radio and TV ad.

If you are Tier B, it will be difficult to get you approved for the incentivized rate, but not impossible. Your credit report will have to show you have at least five years of previous car loans, and that you made every payment on time. Also, you must have no judgments, liens, or charge-offs against you. Plus, you'll most likely be required to put down 20% to 30%. That will relieve a lot of the lending company's liability since they'll be in an equity position in the car you're buying.

With Tier C, you may get approved through the captive finance arm of the manufacturer, but your interest rate will be on the upper end, around 14% to 20%. And that's if you don't have any charge-offs or collections, and no more than two 30-day late pays on your previous auto loan. And any 30-, 60-, or 90-day late pays on your auto loans or credit cards must not be current (within a year.)

Tier D, you're in the dog house. Your credit application gets sent directly to those lending institutions that buy the contracts of high-risk buyers. If you do get approved, there will be a whole lot of stipulations that must be met before the deal is made. You'll have to come up with three to six personal references. You must have their legal names, current addresses and phone numbers. You'll have to bring in your pay stubs from work. You may also need a utility bill sent to your house in your name, and your current bank statement. Once you meet all the requirements, you'll get an interest rate anywhere between 21% and 30%.

THE KISS OF DEATH LIST

These items will give you an immediate turn-down faster than you can cry, "Those aren't mine, they're my ex's!":

1. Federal or state liens.
2. Behind on child support.
3. An open bankruptcy.
4. A discharged bankruptcy but behind on payments of reestablished credit.
5. Being sued.
6. A repossession.
7. A foreclosure.
8. A "skip trace" report.
9. A history of charge-offs and collections.

FORGET IT! All these will show up on your credit report and they are your death knell. You should buy a monthly bus pass instead.

YOU'RE APPROVED!

An important note regarding a 0.0% incentivized rate: If you can pay cash for your new car but you can get a 0% interest rate, TAKE THE

0.0%! Use their money instead of your own to finance it. Here's why: If your car costs $40,000 out the door, you could pay the entire price. But then your personal account will be drained by that much. Instead, just put down the minimum amount required and pay off the balance in monthly installments since you'll pay no interest. It doesn't cost you anything to use their money.

Say the minimum is 10% to qualify. You use $4,000 of your own money and carry a balance of $36,000. Your monthly payments will be $600 for 60 months. Now put the $36,000 you didn't spend into a money market account for 60 months and see how much you have at the end of the term!

If you're like most of us, though, you have to finance. You can borrow money from your bank, credit union, or the captive financial arm of the brand you're buying. If the car you want has interest incentives available, the rate will always be lower through the captive financial arm than through banks and credit unions. If you have a choice of a hefty cash rebate or low interest rate, have the finance manager show you both monthly payments: the incentivized interest rate with $5,000 down and the cash rebate price at the standard interest rates, or at your bank or credit union rate, with the same $5,000 down.

$5,000 is an arbitrary number. I'm using it to make a point. When getting both payments, always use the same amount down. It's the only way you can accurately compare the two. Sometimes a hefty rebate can offset a higher interest rate. Be sure you're getting the lowest payment possible.

At this point, you now know what interest rate you most likely qualified for. Or at least you know what your ceiling will be. You know the final selling price of your new car, including customer or dealer rebates, what your trade-in is worth, and how much out-of-pocket cash you want to put down. The sales manager has already gone over your credit report and sent it to the finance manager to have him look it over. The finance manager has now submitted your contract to the captive financial arm or an outside loan company, waiting for their approval. Once he gets it, he calls you into his office and the paper work begins.

Before I go over the contract with you, you need to know something: Dealerships make money on financing. How much they make depends on what type of house they are. If it's a respectable establishment, you can expect to pay about .5% to 1% over their "buy rate." They're entitled to it to help offset the costs of keeping the doors open and the lights on.

Think of their "buy rate" as the Federal Prime Interest Rate. The Federal Reserve sets the interest rate. Banks pay that amount of interest every time they borrow from them. In turn, they loan you money at a rate higher than the Federal Prime. The type of loan and your strength of credit determines what percentage you'll get charged. But you'll never get a loan at the Prime Interest rate. After all, the bank needs to make money. It has overhead to pay, a land lease, utilities, payroll, and insurance benefits. And there's the cost in hours of labor to do the transfer of funds.

The same holds true for a dealership. It has to pay the finance manager, the sales manager, the salesman, plus costs in labor, electricity, and ink and paper to process your loan application. If you get a 0% or any other incentivized interest rate, there is no bump in the rate. It's already set by the financial institution and they pay a flat rate to the dealer for acquiring the loan. But if the car doesn't offer interest incentives, you should pay no more than 1% over the rate the dealer has to pay.

Most states have a 3% cap over the buy rate. So how do you find out what the dealer's buy rate is? That's very difficult. All dealers want to keep that confidential. But they're not bound by any contract or law to keep it private. If you should call the customer service of the captive financial institution, they won't tell you, either. Because of the Privacy Act, that information must come directly from the dealer. The best way to handle this is to be direct. Politely, and in a businesslike manner, ask the finance manager what your buy rate is. Then watch the reaction on his face. He won't be expecting it. If he gets flustered and gets defensive, tell him you want to know how strong you are. You want to know if you're a Tier A.

Ask him to show you the acceptance notice from the lender. A schlock house finance manager will berate your for asking. He'll get red in the face and will want to throw you out. Before he can do that, leave on your own accord. This guy has something to hide, and that is all the circumstantial evidence you need to know that you're about be had.

A reputable finance manager will be stunned at first. Reassure him that you don't mind paying .5% to 1% over. He needs to make some money for the dealership. By letting him know you're willing to pay something reasonable and fair over the buy rate, it just may get him to release the information to you. Although it's highly unlikely. But you have given him notice that you know much more about financing than the average buyer and you want to be treated honestly and fairly. If you're the type who feels you shouldn't have to pay anything over the buy rate and you never have before, guess what? You have! You've been paying it from the day you bought your very first car! You never knew this because it had never been disclosed to you before. But now you know. Knowledge is power. Intelligent power will get you a fair deal.

CHAPTER 21

The Purchase Contract

Purchasing a car on credit means that you agree to make a monthly payment to the lending company until the loan is paid in full. YOU DO NOT OWN THE CAR while you're paying for it. The loan company does. You are merely borrowing it. That's why you must have full insurance coverage on the car until you pay it off. You are protecting the loan company's property, their collateral.

Once you enter into an agreement to buy a car, you must sign many documents. They run the gamut from the actual contract to disclosure agreements. Disclosures are statements, conditions, and exclusions that protect the dealership and the lending company from any liability should you provide false information or use the vehicle in a way it wasn't designed for. The one exemption to this is the Lemon Law disclosure. It protects you in the event your new car is found to have mechanical, electrical, or safety issues that cannot be resolved by the service department.

Every state has its own contracts and its own number of additional disclosures. There may be tire chain disclosures or infant seat disclosures or another type of disclosure particular to your region. But the one thing every dealer has in common is the FEDERAL TRUTH IN LENDING DISCLOSURES in the sales contract. At the top of the contract is the buyer's (and co-buyer's) full name and address. Next is the dealership's name and address. Then the vehicle information:

1. New or used, year, make, and model.
2. The current actual odometer reading.
3. The vehicle identification number (VIN.)
4. Primary use, business or personal.

Next are the disclosures. Be alert and aware. The finance manager needs to walk you through this, step by step, and explain everything plainly. The first is the Federal Truth in Lending Disclosures, which includes these items:

1. The annual interest rate: the cost of your credit in a yearly percentage rate.
2. The total finance charge: the dollar amount the credit will cost you.
3. Amount financed: the amount of credit provided to you.
4. Total amount of payments: the amount you'll have paid at the end of the term.
5. Total selling price: the total cost of your purchase on credit, including interest and your down-payment.

Next is your payment schedule. This tells you the amount of your payment, how many payments you'll have, the beginning date, and the termination date. The actual itemization of your purchase is next, and includes these items:

1. The total cash price of your car and accessories: the agreed-upon, negotiated price.
2. The cash price of the vehicle.
3. The cash price of accessories.
4. The document preparation fee: the cost of preparing the contract and disclosures, plus transferring ownership of your trade-in.
5. Smog fee—if applicable.
6. Sales tax on the vehicle and accessories.
7. The optional service contract or extended warranty.

8. The prior credit or lease balance the dealer pays to another institution: any amount that you owe on your trade-in, and the lending company to which it's paid.
9. Optional gap insurance: If your car is totaled, it will cover the difference between what your insurance company paid you and the amount you owe.

Next is the total price of all the above amounts, followed by your license fee and any other state or regional fees. These fees are added to the above price to get the Subtotal. After that, you'll have an itemization of your trade-in and/or cash down-payment, along with any applicable cash rebates. The total of all these figures is your Total Amount Financed. Be sure that the total amount financed figure here is the very same as the total amount financed in the Federal Truth in Lending Disclosure. It has to be—otherwise the contract is null and void.

The purchase contract* has several more disclosures. One is the Personal Insurance disclosure where you state you have the required amount of insurance necessary to take delivery of the car.

Another is the Representation of Buyer, which states that you are exactly who you claim to be on the credit application, and that your social security number and driver's license are indeed yours. If any of this information is found to be false, the contract is void and you must bring the car back. You may also be subject to criminal charges.

You'll have to sign a Notice of Rescission Rights which declares that if the dealer cannot get you financed for any reason, it can rescind the contract and you must bring the car back. If this happens, you may have the option of obtaining credit on your own or paying cash for the car instead of returning it. That is determined by the dealer.

The Credit Life Insurance disclosure says the lender will pay off the car in the event of your total disability or death, if you are the principal buyer. Most dealers no longer sell this because they're only involved in the financing of the car, not insuring it.

You'll see another disclosure that states that once you and the dealer representative sign the contract, it cannot be changed without

---

*See a sample of a purchase contract at www.InsidetheMindsofCarDealers.com

the consent of both parties. And lastly, you must sign the No Cooling Off Period statement, acknowledging that you cannot later cancel this contract simply because you changed your mind, decided the vehicle costs too much, or wish you bought another vehicle instead. Most states now require this disclosure to be on the contract. And not just a statement posted on the finance manager's desk.

After you sign that statement, the car is effectively yours. You can only cancel your contract with the agreement of the dealer, or for a legal cause, such as fraud. Some states have the DMV form in the contract; others have it as a separate document. Either way, you'll sign a mileage statement, verifying that the miles shown on your trade-in are true, that you are the true owner, that you release all liability of your trade-in to the dealership, and that you give the dealership power of attorney to complete all the necessary paperwork on your behalf for the transfer of ownership from you to them.

CHAPTER 22

When to Buy Rather Than Lease

Buy a car if:

1. You drive 15,001 miles or more per year.

2. You keep a car for more than three years.

3. You want to customize your car with special paint or accessories.

Leases are for people who drive 15,000 miles or less per year, and keep a car for only two or three years. Leases are designed to give you a major benefit in money down and monthly payments, as well as a tax write-off—but only if you meet this criteria. If you think a four-year lease will maximize your dollars, you are incredibly wrong. A vehicle's depreciation rate is a lot more at four years than it is at three years. The higher the depreciation rate, the higher your monthly payments. The longer the loan, the higher the interest rate on the lease will be.

Custom paint and many accessories cannot be residualized. In plain English, that means if you want $7,200 worth of custom paint and wheels on your car and want a 36-month lease, it will add an additional $200 per month to your lease payment. Then you have to restore it back to original factory condition when you turn it in. That will cost you a bundle too. You might as well buy it. Leasing gives you no benefit in this situation.

CHAPTER 23

The CSI Survey

Now you have your new car in your driveway. The neighbors see it. People passing by admire it. And most importantly, you get a lot of compliments on it. Now you have pride in ownership. The final step in buying a car is near. It's called a Customer Satisfaction Index survey. The manufacturer will send one to you within two to four weeks of your purchase. In it, you must answer questions by checking an appropriate response. THIS SURVEY IS VERY IMPORTANT TO YOUR SALESPERSON! His job depends on it, as well as his income.

If you had a great experience with him, please fill it out! Check every "5" or "Completely Satisfied" on it. If you had a pleasant time with your salesperson but not with the finance or sales manager, please do not give her a lesser mark. Even though your salesperson has nothing to do with the way they treated you, she'll still be penalized by the factory and the dealership, because the CSI survey results do not separate their scores from your salesperson's. It's all attributed only to her.

If you should have a problem with anyone, or anything at the dealer, by all means call your salesperson. Let him know the situation and that you have the CSI survey in your hand.

I'm sure you'll see a very fast resolution to your situation. Then send it in with all high marks. Or if you still can't, please throw it out. As I've mentioned, the dealership and manufacturer put a lot of weight into these results. And it can gravely affect your salesperson's employment status.

If, on the other hand, your salesperson was rude, condescending, a liar, or intolerable, give him what he deserves: all bottom-feed marks. He needs to be fired. It's the only way we can get rid of all the blue-suede-shoes salespeople and clean up our reputation.

NOW YOU KNOW MORE THAN ENOUGH TO BUY YOUR NEXT CAR

One final thought: I sincerely hope you learned a lot from this book and that your next experience at the dealership will be a very pleasant and knowledgeable one. I hope that you will leave in your new car knowing you got the best deal you could get and still let everyone make some money. After all, a dealership is a business.